THE DEVASTATION
OF THE INDIES:
A BRIEF ACCOUNT

¶ Breuissima relacion dla des truycion delas yndias.

Escubrierõ se las yn dias enel año de mil ꝗ quatro ciẽtos ꝛ nouenta ꝛ dos : fueron se a poblar el año siguiente de chꝛistianos espa ñoles / poꝛ manera que ha quarenta ꝛ nueue años que fueron a ellas can tidad de españoles: ꝛ la pꝛimera tierra donde entraron para hecho de poblar: fue la grandeꝛ felicissima ꝛsla es pañola que tiene seꝛsciẽtas leguas en toꝛno. Aꝛ otras muꝛ grandes ꝛ infinitas ꝛslas al rededoꝛ poꝛ todas las partes della: que todas estauan ꝛ las vimos las mas po bladas ꝛ llenas de naturales gẽtes Yndios dellas que puede ser tierra poblada enel mundo. La tierra firme que esta de esta Ysla poꝛ lo mas cercano dozientas ꝛ cin cuenta leguas pocas mas / tiene de costa de mar mas ð diez mil leguas descubiertas ꝛ cada dia se ðscubrẽ mas: todas llenas como vna colmena de gẽtes / enlo que has ta el año de quarenta ꝛ vno se ha descubierto: que pare ce que puso dios en aquellas tierras todo el golpe / o la maꝛoꝛ cantidad de todo el linage humano.

¶ Todas estas vniuersas ꝛ infinitas gentes a toto ge nero crio dios los mas simples sin maldades ni doble zes: obedientissimas: fidelissimas a sus señoꝛes natura les : ꝛ alos chꝛistianos a quien siruen : mas humildes / mas pacientes / mas pacificas ꝛ quietas : sin renzillas

BARTOLOMÉ DE LAS CASAS

THE DEVASTATION OF THE INDIES:
A Brief Account

*Translated from the Spanish
by Herma Briffault*

Introduction by Bill M. Donovan

The Johns Hopkins University Press
Baltimore and London

The Devastation of the Indies: A Brief Account translated from *Tratados I* de
Fray Bartolomé de las Casas © 1965, Fondo de Cultura Economica, Mexico.

English translation © 1974 by The Crossroad Publishing Company
Reprinted by permission
Introduction © 1992 The Johns Hopkins University Press
All rights reserved
Printed in the United States of America on acid-free paper

Johns Hopkins Paperbacks edition, 1992
Fifth impression, 1994

The Johns Hopkins University Press
2715 North Charles Street
Baltimore, Maryland 21218-4319
The Johns Hopkins Press Ltd., London

Library of Congress Cataloging-in-Publication Data

Casas, Bartolomé de las, 1474-1566.
  [Brevísima relación de la destrucción de las Indias. English]
  The devastation of the Indies : a brief account / Bartolomé de las Casas :
translated from the Spanish by Herma Briffault : introduction by Bill M.
Donovan.
    p.   cm.
  Translation of: Brevísima relación de la destrucción de las Indias.
  Originally published: New York : Seabury Press, 1974.
  Includes bibliographical references.
  ISBN 0-8018-4430-4 (pbk.)
  1. Indians, Treatment of–Latin America.   2. Spain–Colonies–
America.   I. Title.
F1411.C43   1992   91-44199

A catalog record for this book is available from the British Library.

" . . . *for in the beginning the Indians regarded
the Spaniards as angels from heaven.*"

CONTENTS

THE DEVASTATION
OF THE INDIES:
A BRIEF ACCOUNT

INTRODUCTION

by Bill M. Donovan

Were I to recount the vile acts committed here, the
exterminations, the massacres, the cruelties, the violence and sinfulness against God and the King of Spain,
I would write a very big book, but this will have to wait
for another time, God willing.

ALTHOUGH IT numbers fewer than one hundred fifty
pages, *The Devastation of the Indies: A Brief Account* was
a big book when published in 1552, and remains so today.
Its appearance in Seville created an immediate sensation.
Bartolomé de Las Casas's exposé of Spanish mistreatment
of Amerindians produced public outrage that was directed
at both the conquistadors who were committing the atrocities
and at the writer who had made them public. Las Casas
offered a firsthand account of Europe's earliest colonization

1

of the Americas from the unique vantage of a participant. He began as a soldier. Revolted by the cruelties he saw being inflicted on native peoples, he became the early modern era's most articulate defender of Indian rights.

Yet *The Devastation of the Indies* did not long remain a parochial story of the Spaniards and the Indians. It was almost immediately translated into every major European language, whereupon it provided one of the ideological foundations of English, French, and Dutch attempts to break the Iberian monopoly on American colonization. Las Casas's revelations seriously undermined the Spanish moral claim to the Americas. Indeed, *The Devastation of the Indies* has served as one basis for the so-called Black Legend, which sought to discredit Spain's American involvement by painting all Spanish activities and the Spanish national character in the most cruel and negative light. Even today the Black Legend heavily influences Northern European and North American perceptions of Latin American history and culture.[1]

Las Casas's account also helped spur a much deeper debate on the subject of Western/non-Western relations. Discussion of the nature of Europe's historical contact with non-Western peoples, together with questions over the enormous demographic and cultural catastrophe Las Casas described, has made him and his essay the center of passionate controversy. The five hundredth anniversary of Columbus's landfall offers a particularly propitious moment for reissuing Las Casas's text. Plans to celebrate the Columbus quincentenary have already aroused heated debate in North and Latin America over the meaning of Europe's arrival in the Americas and its consequences for native peoples and cultures.

The systematic destruction of the rain forests and the continuing murder of their remaining native populations make Las Casas's work quite relevant to contemporary concerns. Spanish devastation of the Indies will be part of every phase of this debate.

The issues raised four and a half centuries ago remain without resolution today: Should Indians have the same rights as European Americans? Do they have intrinsic rights to their land and culture? How have Christian humanism and Western notions of rationality responded to non-Western cultures? To what extent did the eradication of non-Western populations and cultures corrupt Western values?

Little is known about Las Casas's early life and family background. He was born in Seville in 1484.[2] His father, Pedro de Las Casas, was a merchant who became sufficiently wealthy to permit his son to study Latin instead of entering the family business. Las Casas's father and three of his uncles accompanied Columbus on his second voyage, but no information survives about their activity in the Indies. We do know, however, that Columbus gave a young Indian slave to Pedro de Las Casas, who in turn gave the Indian boy to his son as a companion. Bartolomé returned him to the authorities so that he could be repatriated to the Indies. At the age of eighteen, in 1502, Las Casas left Spain with twenty-five hundred other eager adventurers bound for the Indies on Nicolás de Ovando's fleet. In 1506 or 1507 he returned to Europe to be ordained a deacon in Rome, leaving soon thereafter for the Indies again, where, in 1512, he became the first priest to be ordained in the New World.

Hispaniola in the early sixteenth century was a violent

place. Its gold fields offered quick wealth and its native population freely exploitable labor. The Spanish crown had sent Ovando to reestablish royal authority and ensure the proper operation of the *repartimiento,* an allocation of Indians to individuals known as *encomenderos.* When the Spanish Conquest extended to Mexico and South America the system became known as *encomienda.* In return for the use of native labor, the crown instructed *encomenderos* to take adequate care of Indians and instruct them in civilized behavior, but the arrangement almost immediately degenerated into virtual slavery.

During his first couple of years in the Indies, Las Casas met some of the most celebrated leaders of the conquest, including Hernando Cortés and Pedro de Alvarado. He also took the time to learn several native languages. As a chaplain, he accompanied Diego de Velásquez and Pánfilo de Narváz on the conquest of Cuba. In reward for his service, Las Casas received Indians and land. By all appearances he had settled in to become a typical *encomendero.*

In 1514, however, Las Casas surprised his parishioners by preaching a Pentecost Sunday sermon severely condemning Spanish treatment of native people. He soon freed his own native slaves and began vigorously interceding with local authorities on the Indians' behalf. For years, historians thought that a sudden religious experience had transformed Las Casas into a defender of Indians. We now know that his conversion occurred gradually over the course of a year or more, as he became increasingly disenchanted with the entire structure of Spanish/Indian relations.[3]

Las Casas eventually realized that the real solution for

Indian mistreatment lay not just with challenging the conduct of individual *encomenderos* but also in calling into question the entire system of *encomienda* and its relationship to Christian morality. He ceaselessly denounced the officials who oversaw Spain's American outposts and who slaughtered and enslaved thousands of natives for their own financial benefit. Such subversion earned him powerful enemies among local officials and *encomenderos,* who bitterly complained to influential individuals in Spain.

Las Casas made little headway in his crusade until 1520, when Charles V (of the Holy Roman Empire—Charles I of Spain) granted him a hearing to explain his views and defend himself against the charges colonial Spaniards had laid on him. In a chamber filled with members of the royal council, together with supporters and opponents of native rights, Las Casas argued that the period for military conquest of the Indians had passed. Now, he claimed, was the time for peaceful conversion of natives and the promotion of agricultural colonization. He hardly stood alone in condemning Spanish cruelties against Indians. Other voices had begun to sound in the Americas. Antonio de Montesinos had begun denouncing the treatment of Indians even before Las Casas. Juan Quevedo, the Bishop of Darien, returned to Spain in about 1520 to protest the behavior of colonial officials. A small but influential group of royal ministers and Spanish churchmen supported the general proposition of protecting Indians. After heated debate, Charles V came down on the side of Las Casas, ruling that the Indies could be governed without the force of arms. Yet the ruling had little practical effect in the distant Indies.

During the next quarter century, Las Casas mostly suffered defeats in his efforts to defend America's native populations. In 1520 he left Spain to establish a settlement in Venezuela, hoping to peacefully convert local Indians and, at the same time, create an economically self-sufficient community. But opposition from *encomenderos* and colonial officials helped incite an Indian rebellion that wrecked the project. Desolate over its failure, he entered the Dominican order as a monk in 1522. The years that followed were ones of intellectual growth and personal frustration for Las Casas. He set out his proposal of peaceful conversion as an alternative to military conquest in *Del único modo de atraer a todos los pueblos a la verdadera religión* (The Only Method of Attracting Everyone to the True Religion).[4] While in the monastery, he began his monumental *Apologética historia de las Indias* and the *Historia de las Indias* and continued a life-long passion for collecting documents. One of Las Casas's critics charged that he once arrived in Tlaxcala, Mexico, "with twenty-seven or thirty-seven [Indian] carriers—and the greatest part of what they were carrying was accusations against the Spaniards, and other rubbish."[5]

Although colonial Spaniards scorned any attempt to ameliorate the Indians' plight, moral encouragement arrived from Europe in the form of Pope Paul III's bull *Sublimis Deus* (1537), proclaiming that the American Indians were rational beings with souls and that their lives and property should be protected. During that same year, Charles V supported an effort by Las Casas and the Dominicans to establish missions in Guatemala, based on the precepts laid out in *Del único modo*. The high point of the crown's efforts came in 1542 with the so called *Leyes Nuevas* (New Laws), which forbade Indian slavery and sought to end the *encomienda* system within a generation by outlawing the transference of *encomiendas* through family inheritance. Las Casas, who was in Spain at the time, directly influenced the direction of the New Laws, in part by reading the first version of *The Devastation of the Indies* to a horrified royal court.

In 1544 he returned to the Indies for a brief and tempestuous tenure as the Bishop of Chiapas. He had been offered the post of Bishop of Peru, the most prestigious post in the colonies; but, in keeping with his character, he turned it down to preside over one of the poorest areas in New Spain. Proclamation of the New Laws brought outright revolt in parts of Spanish America and fierce antagonism everywhere. When Las Casas denied final absolution to any Spaniard who refused to free his Indians or pay restitution, he received threats against his life. Clergy who had ties to *encomenderos* defied him. Las Casas had made preparations to return to Spain when, in 1545, colonial opposition persuaded Charles V to revoke key inheritance statutes in the New Laws. Before leaving, however, Las Casas issued a confessor manual for the priests in his diocese. His *Confesionario* produced public outrage by reiterating that all Spaniards seeking absolution must free their Indians and make restitution, even if the Indians were part of a deeded estate. Las Casas justified his decision by arguing that all wealth acquired through *encomiendas* was ill gotten, declaring, "There is no Spaniard in the Indies who has shown good faith in connection with the wars of Conquest."[6]

Such a claim denoted more than another attack on the

encomienda system; it struck at the very basis of Spain's legitimacy in the Americas. It asserted that, because the Spanish had extracted all their wealth by using Indians, the sum of their American activities since Columbus's arrival was unjust and, by logical extension, so was Spain's American presence. Not surprisingly, officials confiscated *Confesionario*. The Council of the Indies, which directed colonial activities from Spain, recalled Las Casas to Spain in 1547.

In Europe, Las Casas had to contend with a new and potentially more dangerous challenge to his campaign for native rights. Juan Ginés de Sepúlveda—one of Spain's leading humanists, who possessed not only an impressive intellect but also formidable friends at court—mounted an intellectual defense of aggression against American Indians, based on the doctrine of just war. Las Casas vigorously condemned Sepúlveda's arguments while repeatedly describing the atrocities being committed in the Indies. The Council of the Indies responded to Las Casas's criticisms by recommending to Charles V that all New World conquests be halted until a meeting of jurists and theologians could determine "how conquests may be conducted justly and with security of conscience."[7] In April 1550, Charles V ordered a meeting of the two men, to debate the merits of just wars and Aristotelian logic in regard to American Indians.

Much popular misconception has surrounded the "great debate" between Las Casas and Sepúlveda. It took place in the northern Spanish city of Valladolid in 1550.[8] The two men never met in face-to-face debate but instead stated their cases individually before the court. Sepúlveda built his three-hour defense of just wars against Indians, and the necessity of Spain's having waged them, on four points. First, the Indians had committed grave sins by their idolatry and sins against nature. Second, the Indians' "natural rudeness and inferiority" accorded with the Aristotelian notion that some men were born natural slaves. Third, military conquest formed the most efficacious method of converting Indians to Christianity. Last, conquering Indians made it possible to protect the weak amongst them. In rebuttal, Las Casas took five days to read his *Apologéticia historia*. In the end the majority of judges sided with Las Casas but, perhaps fearing controversy, refused to render a public decision. Legislation by the crown continued to move slowly toward the abolition of Indian slavery and of the worst features of the *encomienda* system.

In August 1550 Las Casas resigned the Chiapas bishopric, assuming residency in the Dominican San Gregorio monastery, where he churned out a remarkable series of publications and completed manuscripts he had begun earlier. In 1552, without seeking clearance from the Inquisition, Las Casas published *The Devastation of the Indies*. Normally, such conduct would have provoked severe penalties against author and publisher, but Las Casas's prestige protected both from official punishment. In Spain and Spanish America his critics accused him of treason, but the work awakened the rest of Catholic and Protestant Europe to Spanish atrocities, and French, Dutch, and English translations quickly appeared.

Las Casas completed his two largest works during these years. The first, *Apologética historia,* which is anthropological in character, argued for the rationality of American natives by favorably comparing them to the Greeks and Romans. The second, the *Historia de las Indias,* begun in the 1520s, eventually ran to three volumes. Both works sought to prove the error of Spanish assumptions of their innate superiority over the Indians. Despite its stated partiality, *Historia* supplies much of what is today known about Columbus and the early stages of Spanish colonization in the Americas.

Las Casas, in his declining years, remained an advocate for Indian rights. His last great success occurred during the final years of the 1550s, when Peruvian conquistadors offered millions of ducats to Phillip II in exchange for perpetual *encomiendas.* Las Casas adroitly had the decision postponed while he gained the power of attorney that enabled him to officially act on the Indians' behalf. Las Casas guaranteed that Peruvian Indians could collect enough silver to outbid the conquistadors, and, in the end, the attempted bribe failed and the conquistadors withdrew their offer.

Such victories notwithstanding, his last years were not happy. Hectoring for native rights made Las Casas an unpopular figure at court. He remained uncompromising, insisting that the Spanish make complete restitution for their sins in the Americas, and decried the continuing offenses against natives in the Indies. He fought with other clerics as well on the proper means to Christianize Indians. All of his activity proceeded urgently; he believed God might well destroy Spain for its sins. Las Casas worked until the last days of his life to help protect Indians from Spanish *en-*

comenderos. On the day of his death, in July 1566, he voiced regret for not having done more. He lies in the convent chapel of Our Lady of Atocha in Madrid.

The enduring relevance of Las Casas's *Devastation of the Indies* lies in its presentation of timeless and universal issues of human rights. Yet, consideration of the context in which this work appeared remains fundamentally important, for Las Casas and his public reception clearly reflected the intellectual and moral climate of the sixteenth century. It is hardly possible to overstate the astonishment that the discoveries made by Columbus and the early Spanish conquistadors caused among Europeans. Their minds had to assimilate the sudden appearance of a vast "New World," one profoundly different from that which Western intellectual and religious traditions had created.

Sixteenth-century Europeans sailed out into the world armed with knowledge from the ancients, above all Aristotle; with a long tradition of exotic European travel literature filled with strange people, fantastic geography, and mythic creatures; and with the Bible. From these texts, Europeans had constructed a complete cosmology, one that explained how the world had begun, how it would end, the types of people—good and evil—who had once inhabited the world, and the types of people still in it. Nowhere in that system did space exist for the variety of life they encountered in the Americas. They had no preparation for lethal snakes that warned their victims before striking, shaggy cowlike creatures in herds that covered the horizon, or spherical fish armed with paralyzing stingers. Yet they somehow had to make sense of what they saw before them, using the intellectual tools at hand.

The notion of an earthly paradise, a Garden of Eden, existing somewhere over the horizon, held a prominent place in the hearts and minds of Renaissance travelers. In part, the notion was born of dismal living conditions in Europe and the widespread feeling that Western society had lost its spiritual bearings. Not surprisingly, many of the earliest visitors to America wrote that they had arrived in paradise. The land enthralled and astonished early Spanish and Portuguese explorers. They praised its climate, marveled at the colorful animals, birds, and wild fruit.[9] The vastness of America's territory gave rise to fantastic reports of fountains of youth, mountains of gold, tribes of women warriors, and fabulously wealthy white kings. Spanish encounters with the Aztecs and Incas, together with their discovery of a veritable mountain of silver at Potosí, continued to fuel such stories. Throughout the sixteenth and seventeenth centuries, bands of Europeans continued to trek inland searching for El Dorado. Early European voyagers soon realized, however, that Columbus had discovered not paradise but a new continent, one larger than they could have imagined. Moreover, they learned that the idyllic panoramas of the Americas hid an environment full of difficulties and dangers. Reptiles, spiders, and swarms of mosquitoes joined with a searing heat to frustrate attempts at colonization.

The strange inhabitants of this new world posed the greatest intellectual (and practical) challenge. Europeans were shocked to encounter people of whom the Bible and ancient texts made no mention and whose physical appearance clearly differed from that of the Africans and Asians they had expected to find. The earliest Spanish and Portuguese accounts focus on the Indians' innocent childlike appearance: "People began to come to the beach, as naked as their mothers bore them," Columbus wrote. "They are friendly and well-dispositioned people who bare no arms except for small spears. I know that they are a people who can be made free and converted to our Holy Faith more by love than by force."[10] The Spanish further determined that native labor offered the most immediate path to individual wealth. Indian natives could build the houses, tend the fields, and work in the mines, while the conquistadors gained the fortune that had drawn them to the Americas. Yet exploitation of native labor does not account for the systematic commission of atrocities against American Indians that Las Casas describes.

The Spaniards' treatment of the Indians defies tidy explanations. On the one hand, the epic experience of the *Reconquista*—the Iberian military struggle against the Moorish occupation lasting from 711 to 1492—well prepared the Spanish to fight and conquer enemies under extremely difficult conditions. A dynamic martial spirit, medieval in its formation and aggressively religious and aristocratic in attitude, permeated Spanish culture. Many of the Spaniards who chose to migrate to the Indies at the very beginning of the fifteenth century were imbued with that medieval warrior mentality. Conquest and governance are distinct, however, and by the time *The Devastation of the Indies* was printed, the conquest of the Indies had largely been accomplished, in some areas decades before.

Spain found itself profoundly unprepared for the tasks and responsibilities of governing an extended overseas empire. The *Reconquista* had left it with an inchoate administrative system, a backward economy, an impoverished treasury, and a society fractured by the diversity of its linguistic, religious, ethnic, and regional customs. Moreover, at the same time the Spanish were laboring to construct a rational colonial structure, dynastic entanglements had dragged them into Western Europe's religious and political struggles. No models existed for administering overseas possessions. The Spanish had to determine by trial and error the number, type, and training of royal officials. Although their experience in the Canary Islands and the Portuguese experience in Madeira provided prototypes for establishing a plantation economy, the fundamental questions of what the Americas were to be and what the proper relationship between Indians and Europeans should be remained unanswered during Las Casas's time.

The practical problems of governing a distant and culturally remote empire postponed or made secondary any consideration of native rights. Wooden sailing ships made for slow and inconsistent communication between Europe and the Indies. Royal authorities remained out of touch with colonial officials for months at a stretch. Thus, they literally had no idea of events in the colonies or to what extent the crown's representatives were fulfilling their duties. Even the most competent colonial officials found that the vast distances within the Americas impeded the enforcement of royal policy. Colonists realized they virtually had carte blanche in imposing their will on their immediate environment.

Las Casas offers the example of a band of thirty Spaniards who entered an area of Yucatan that had been reserved for Franciscan missionaries. Although the viceroy ordered them to leave, the conquistadors refused. Their actions then almost led to the missionaries' death. Yet, even after the viceroy had officially declared them traitors, the conquistadors continued persecuting local Indians, since their distance from the viceroy, who resided in New Spain (modern Mexico), made them immune to royal sanctions.

Spaniards' behavior toward non-Westerners in the New World followed a medieval tradition that was based on their contacts with the Moors. It allowed them to rationalize the entire spectrum of European/Indian relations, and it did not precisely define the limits for using violence and coercion. In 1452 the church had begun encouraging Iberian expansion by issuing a series of papal bulls and briefs granting the Portuguese, and later the Spanish, a broad combination of rights and privileges in exchange for promoting missionary activity. The papacy empowered the two crowns to conquer and even enslave pagans "inimical to the name of Christ."[11] Such papal edicts assumed that the people whom the Spanish and Portuguese would encounter already had some acquaintance with Christianity and that these nonbelievers were responding to the true faith by either ignoring it or actively opposing missionary activity. Spaniards in the Indies claimed that the bulls gave them the right to use just war to convert local populations who had refused to immediately accept Christianity. Thus, responsibility for enslavement of Indians was placed on the Indians themselves. After learning of the true situation in the New World, both the crown and the church rejected such assertions. They pointed out that, unlike the Moors, Amerindians had had no acquaintance with Christianity before Columbus. To underscore the duplicity of the conquistadors' argument, critics such as Las Casas exposed the common practices of deliberately preaching to the Indians' out of their earshot and in languages foreign to local tribes.

The peaceable Arawaks, whom Columbus encountered, offered not even the flimsiest pretext for just war. Other native peoples, the Caribs of the Lesser Antilles, for example, strengthened the conquistadors' claims of justification by stiffly resisting the Spanish. The European confrontation with the Aztecs did the most to fuel arguments that American Indians were essentially barbarians. The Aztecs' practice of human sacrifice genuinely horrified the Spanish and led some to believe "if God could live in the Indies so could the devil." It raised the question of how any people who engaged in such bloodthirst could be considered civilized and rational. Yet Las Casas so argued in his "Defense of Human Sacrifice," by comparing Indian culture to ancient European civilizations. He used Aristotle's theory of probable error to exonerate their behavior, claiming, "the ancient history of both pagans and Catholics testifies that almost all peoples used to do the same thing."

Much discussion of *The Devastation of the Indies* has focused on Las Casas's accuracy and therefore his credibility as a historian and social critic. Opponents have charged him with producing anti-Spanish propaganda. Although this was not his intent, English, Dutch, and French translations of

The Devastation of the Indies, complete with lurid illustrations of Spanish atrocities, did furnish Spain's rivals with abundant ammunition for attacking its claims on the New World. The English were perhaps the most active in using Las Casas's writings to condemn the Spanish. As late as 1898 Americans used his accounts as a rationale for eliminating Spain's presence in the Americas.[12] Critics who made reference to him invariably cited Las Casas's position as a bishop and as an eyewitness participant in the conquest as evidence of the text's veracity. Conversely, defenders of Spain, such as Ramón Menéndez Pidal, have charged that *The Devastation of the Indies* completely exaggerates both the misdeeds of the conquistadors and the virtues of the Indians.

In addressing the question of Las Casas's credibility, one must note that certain internal assumptions shaped the manner in which *The Devastation of the Indies* was written and intended to be received. Las Casas directed his manuscript specifically to Charles V, and not, initially, toward the general public. Because he sought to sway the opinion and emotions of the king of Spain, the Holy Roman emperor, Las Casas constructed a Manichaean argument in which he divided the New World into good Indians and malicious Spaniards.

Although the binary character of Las Casas's logic resulted in oversimplification, it furnished an elegantly rational structure for his argument by forcing Charles V into an either/or situation: If the king accepted Las Casas's argument he would be a Christian prince who would end the terrible abuses committed in his overseas dominions. On the other hand, if he rejected the argument, he would be a tyrant. To enhance this impression, Las Casas repeatedly used the word *tyrants* to describe colonial officials who were oppressing Indians.

Any appraisal of Las Casas as a historian must begin with the question How many Indians died at Spanish hands? According to Las Casas, Spanish conquistadors killed millions of Indians through enslavement and outright murder. Critics have accused him of flagrant embellishment, if not total invention, in his calculations. Much of that criticism has been based on the view that Las Casas grossly overestimated the number of natives living in the Americas before Europeans arrived. This view asserts that the Spanish could not possibly have killed or enslaved as many Indians as Las Casas claimed, because the entire native population never approached the magnitude he suggested. While Las Casas often created contradictory calculations, recent studies have produced estimates of pre-Columbian populations and post-conquest declines that support his description of demographic catastrophe.[13] Las Casas emerges far more as a representative of the statistical imprecision of his time than as an individual who deliberately falsified the evidence.

Las Casas's thesis of good Indians versus avaricious Spaniards does indicate his lack of knowledge. By holding individual Spaniards responsible for the entire spectrum of destruction in the Americas, Las Casas overlooked the role European and African diseases played in decimating native populations. The biological attack that accompanied and, at times, preceded European penetration of American shores and hinterlands constituted the single most important component in the eventual European conquest of the Western Hemisphere. Pandemics not only killed millions of Amerindians, they violently overturned the social and psychological foundations of native cultures. Without the debilitating ally of disease, the West's acquisition of the Americas would have resembled Britain's occupation of India or the French empire in Indochina: a numerically insignificant European ruling class astride huge culturally autonomous local populations.

Also, it is striking that Las Casas slighted the thousands of Indian allies who aided Cortés and other conquistadors. Small groups of Europeans had little difficulty in subduing primitive tribes such as the Arawaks. Conquering advanced civilizations such as the Aztecs, however, presented a completely different challenge, in which European weapons and tactics alone were insufficient to accomplish the task. Without the thousands of Tlaxcalan warriors who eagerly joined the quest to overthrow the Aztec yoke, Cortés could never have successfully besieged the Aztec capital of Tenochtitlán, the advantage of cannon and horses notwithstanding.

Las Casas would never have claimed to be an impartial observer of the events he described, but did his explicit and unequivocal support of native rights lead him into blanket condemnation of the conquistadors' activities? Did he distort the basic character of Spanish endeavors in America? There can be no doubt that the cruelties he denounced occurred on a large scale. Luis Sánchez's 1566 letter to the president of the Council of the Indies corroborates the Las Casas account.[14] Nonetheless his one-dimensional portrayals of evil Spaniards and moral natives render any detached discussion of Spain's colonial experience difficult. Las Casas, and many of his modern supporters, oversimplify the cultural differences among native tribes. It is hard to feel sympathetic for Aztecs who were arguably as ruthlessly brutal conquerors as were the Spanish.

Las Casas was far more successful as a chronicler of Spanish misdeeds than as a true social critic. He cannot properly be said to have been a social reformer. Characterizing colonial society as a set of extremes renders Las Casas unable to establish any coherent alternative to the economic and political exploitation he condemns. Were there other ways Spanish colonial society could have developed? Las Casas believed that Indians should be peacefully converted to Christianity, but he left open what manner of society could be expected to emerge if they did accept European religion. As many observers have noted, a desperate tone underlies much of his writing in *The Devastation of the Indies* and elsewhere. Part of that desperation comes, of course, from indignation, but part comes from the lack of any genuine plan of reform that might have transformed the colonial regime as it then stood. He supported armed Indian resistance as just war, but given that the Europeans inevitably defeated the native armies, armed struggle did not stand as a viable option. Early in his career, Las Casas, like many other church critics of Indian slavery, suggested that the Spanish substitute African slavery for native labor. He later recanted that proposal, but the retraction never saw public light.

It particularly concerned Las Casas that Spaniards felt they were not accountable for their actions. The Spanish in the New World behaved as though they were accountable to no ecclesiastical or royal authority, and their military advantage made them unbeatable by local natives. Hence, conquistadors ignored priests, disregarded royal orders, and, "as lions, and tigers, hungry for a long time," devoured the lamblike Indians. They needed external restraint, which Las Casas felt had to come from the king.

Las Casas indicted individuals for the New World's problems. Although he saw the *encomienda* system as inherently wicked, it was still colonists—not the king, Spain, or Christian Europe—whom he found responsible for the evil committed under its guise. The suggestion never arises, for example, that Indians just be left alone. Christian responsibility, for Las Casas, meant exposing native people to Grace. Indeed, Indians could not be left alone: they were, to use his phrase, good enough to be Christians and to be integrated into Christian society.

Yet, what did it mean to be a Christian? Las Casas implies that that was unclear to Spaniards living in the Americas, but it was clear to him: he was a Christian opposed to Christianity as it existed in the New World. Yet Las Casas opposed the practices of superficial mass conversion and conversion by force; he proclaimed that real baptism could take place only over time and through peaceful conversion.

The huge black shadow of evil that hangs over *The Devastation of the Indies* is one of the timeless aspects of Las Casas's testimony. Reading the book starkly confronts one with the horrors that occurred in the initial encounters between Europeans and Amerindians. The power of evil emerges as act after act is described by an eyewitness. Las

Casas goes beyond describing events to deal metaphysically with evil. He gives living voice to the screech of God: I am a Spaniard, a Christian Spaniard, and I must testify. All are repelled by scenes of children being fed to dogs. The history of overseas discovery and colonization leaves no doubt that imperial powers generally have acted brutally toward native peoples. Yet, after twentieth-century fire-bombing of civilian targets, after the Holocaust, after the gulags, we cannot simply ascribe these acts to the Spanish or the evils of colonialism.

A strain of anger and hatred pervades the text, and Las Casas has often been accused of hating all Spaniards. He does not hesitate, however, to condemn German adventurers in Venezuela who also tyrannized natives. Spaniards serve as the chief villains because it was mainly they who populated the Indies. It would be more logical to ask how Las Casas could have avoided hating his fellow Spaniards. There is clear evidence in the text of self-hatred for his own earlier behavior. But just as clearly, he still believed in the power of Christian redemption and the power of personal choice to repudiate such behavior.

Images of hell and the final judgment loom large in Las Casas's thinking. A fundamental helplessness in the face of evil is apparent throughout the text. Where does the final judgment for such misdeeds lie? With Las Casas's pre-Enlightenment world view, the only authorities he can think of are the king and God. For that reason he has an apocalyptic vision of the world, believing that people are going to hell for their sins against the Indians.

The essential question asked by *The Devastation of the*

Indies sounds as loudly today as when Las Casas posed it: what is the proper moral reaction to monstrous injustice? How does one react to that injustice when its victims are culturally and geographically distant? What is the proper relation between civilization and barbarism? For the modern reader, *The Devastation of the Indies* raises the profound question whether something intrinsically immoral in the West's ethos has underlain all Western/non-Western relations from the earliest voyages of discovery. Spain's experience in the Americas was in many ways unique. Detailed knowledge about the fatal encounter between Europeans and Amerindians remains because the Spanish (and to a lesser extent the Portuguese in Brazil) openly debated the morality of those relations and enacted legislation to halt the abuses. The repeated circumvention of those laws has tended to overshadow their making, as if they were just an empty exercise. The irony of this situation is that no English, Dutch, French, or North American historical equivalent of Las Casas, nor for that matter of a ruler like Charles V, exists. The Black Legend survives in part because groups such as the Puritans never truly questioned the basic character of European/Indian relations. In the European invasion of North America, native peoples became defined as fundamentally alien, unworthy of any genuine effort to either appreciate their culture or incorporate it at the most peripheral edge of Western society. As a consequence, the Spanish episode in the Indies has powerfully deflected consideration of the morality of other European/American encounters.

Las Casas also asks whether the final judgment lies with history. If so, where are the limits of responsibility? Are we

Columbus's heirs? If we are the inheritors of the past, how do we deal with this historical tragedy—abstractly, in an intellectual setting, or concretely in our relations with other peoples?

NOTES TO THE INTRODUCTION

This introduction was first read to the Loyola College, Baltimore, humanities reading group. I would like to thank William Desmond, Thomas R. Fitzgerald, S.J., Greg Jones, Paul Lukacs, Joseph Walsh, and the rest of the group for their suggestions and insightful comments.

1. Charles Gibson, ed., *The Black Legend: Anti-Spanish Attitudes in the Old World and the New* (New York, 1971) remains the best English introduction to the subject.

2. The year 1474 has traditionally been cited for Las Casas's birth. However, recent scholarship has disproved this earlier date. See Helen Brand Parish and Harold E. Weidman, S.J., "The Correct Birthdate of Bartolomé de Las Casas," *Hispanic American Historical Review* 56, no. 3 (August 1976): 385–403; Marianne Mahn-Lot, *Bartolomé de Las Casas et le droit des Indiens* (Paris, 1982), pp. 11–15. Good biographical sketches of Las Casas are found in Juan Friede and Benjamin Keen, eds., *Bartolomé de Las Casas in History: Toward an Understanding of the Man and His Work* (Dekalb, Ill., 1971) and George Sanderlin, ed., *Bartolomé de Las Casas: A Selection of His Writings* (New York, 1971).

3. Demetrio Ramos Pérz, "La conversión de Las Casas en Cuba: El clérigo y Diego Velazquez," *Estudios sobre Bartolomé de Las Casas* (Seville, 1974), pp. 247–57; Alberto M. Salas, *Tres Cronistas de Indias,* rev. ed. (Mexico City, 1986), p. 184.

4. This work was left unpublished until the twentieth century.

5. Leslie Byrd Simpson, *The Encomienda in New Spain: The Beginning of Spanish Mexico* (Berkeley, 1950), pp. 237–38.

6. Quoted in *Bartolomé de Las Casas, A Selection of His Writings,* ed. and trans. George Sanderlin (New York, 1971), p. 184. The Spaniards Las Casas had in mind were "conquistadors . . . [and] settlers who hold Indians in encomiendas and who by another name are called encomenderos

. . . [and] merchants, not all merchants but those who carried arms and goods to the men who were conquering or warring on Indians, thus becoming participants" (p. 183).

7. Lewis Hanke, *Aristotle and the American Indians: A Study in Race Prejudice in the Modern World* (London, 1959), p. 36.

8. Hanke, *Aristotle and the American Indians,* and Lewis Hanke, *The Spanish Struggle for Justice in the Conquests of America* (Boston, 1965) are the standard secondary works on the topic, and I have largely followed Hanke's interpretation. Readers may also want to refer to Stafford Poole's fine translation, *In Defense of the Indians. The Defense of the Most Reverend Lord, Don Fray Bartolomé de Las Casas, of the Order of Preachers, Late Bishop of Chiapa, Against the Persecutors and Slanderers of the Peoples of the New World Discovered Across the Seas* (DeKalb, Ill., 1974).

9. Christopher Columbus, *The Log of Christopher Columbus,* ed. Robert Fuson (Camden, Maine, 1987), entry of October 17, 1492, pp. 83–84. See too *Carta da Vaz de Caminha,* written in 1500 by a participant in the first European voyage to Brazil. An extended translation may be found in *A Documentary History of Brazil,* ed. E. Branford Burns (New York, 1966), pp. 20–29.

10. Columbus, *Log,* October 12, 1493, p. 76.

11. Quoted in C. R. Boxer, *The Church Militant and Iberian Expansion, 1440–1770* (Baltimore, 1978), p. 30.

12. Gibson's introduction to *The Black Legend* remains the best synopsis of the controversy. See also Juan Comas, "Historical Reality and the Detractors of Father Las Casas," in *Bartolomé de Las Casas in History,* ed. Friede and Keen, pp. 487–537.

13. William M. Denevan, ed., *The Native Population of the Americas in 1492* (Madison, 1976); Woodrow Borah and Sherburne F. Cook, *The Aboriginal Population of Central Mexico on the Eve of the Spanish Conquest* (Berkeley, 1963).

14. Luis Sánchez, "Memorial to President Espinosa, 1566," in *The Black Legend,* ed. Gibson, pp. 90–96.

THE DEVASTATION
OF THE INDIES:
A BRIEF ACCOUNT

by *Bartolomé de Las Casas*

THE INDIES[1] were discovered in the year one thousand four hundred and ninety-two. In the following year a great many Spaniards went there with the intention of settling the land. Thus, forty-nine years have passed since the first settlers penetrated the land, the first so-claimed being the large and most happy isle called Hispaniola,[2] which is six hundred leagues in circumference. Around it in all directions are many other islands, some very big, others very small, and all of them were, as we saw with our own eyes, densely populated with native peoples called Indians. This large island was perhaps the most densely populated place in the world. There must be close to two hundred leagues of land on this island, and the seacoast has been explored for more than ten thousand leagues, and each day more of it is being explored. And all the land so far discovered is a beehive of people; it is as though God had crowded into these lands the great majority of mankind.

Indians →

And of all the infinite universe of humanity, these people are the most guileless, the most devoid of wickedness and duplicity, the most obedient and faithful to their native masters and to the Spanish Christians whom they serve. They are by nature the most humble, patient, and peaceable, holding no grudges, free from embroilments, neither excitable nor quarrelsome. These people are the most devoid of rancors, hatreds, or desire for vengeance of any people in the world. And because they are so weak and complaisant, they are less able to endure heavy labor and soon die of no matter what malady. The sons of nobles among us, brought up in the enjoyments of life's refinements, are no more delicate than are these Indians, even those among them who are of the lowest rank of laborers. They are also poor people, for they not only possess little but have no desire to possess worldly goods. For this reason they are not arrogant, embittered, or greedy. Their repasts are such that the food of the holy fathers in the desert can scarcely be more parsimonious, scanty, and poor. As to their dress, they are generally naked, with only their pudenda covered somewhat. And when they cover their shoulders it is with a square cloth no more than two varas in size.[3] They have no beds, but sleep on a kind of matting or else in a kind of suspended net called *hamacas*. They are very clean in their persons, with alert, intelligent

28

minds, docile and open to doctrine, very apt to receive our holy Catholic faith, to be endowed with virtuous customs, and to behave in a godly fashion. And once they begin to hear the tidings of the Faith, they are so insistent on knowing more and on taking the sacraments of the Church and on observing the divine cult that, truly, the missionaries who are here need to be endowed by God with great patience in order to cope with such eagerness. Some of the secular Spaniards who have been here for many years say that the goodness of the Indians is undeniable and that if this gifted people could be brought to know the one true God they would be the most fortunate people in the world.

Yet into this sheepfold, into this land of meek outcasts there came some Spaniards who immediately behaved like ravening wild beasts, wolves, tigers, or lions that had been starved for many days. And Spaniards have behaved in no other way during the past forty years, down to the present time, for they are still acting like ravening beasts, killing, terrorizing, afflicting, torturing, and destroying the native peoples, doing all this with the strangest and most varied new methods of cruelty, never seen or heard of before, and to such a degree that this Island of Hispaniola, once so populous (having a population that I estimated to be more than three millions), has now a population of barely two hundred persons.

The island of Cuba is nearly as long as the distance between Valladolid and Rome; it is now almost completely depopulated. San Juan[4] and Jamaica are two of the largest, most productive and attractive islands; both are now deserted and devastated. On the northern side of Cuba and Hispaniola lie the neighboring Lucayos[5] comprising more than sixty islands including those called *Gigantes,* beside numerous other islands, some small some large. The least felicitous of them were more fertile and beautiful than the gardens of the King of Seville. They have the healthiest lands in the world, where lived more than five hundred thousand souls; they are now deserted, inhabited by not a single living creature. All the people were slain or died after being taken into captivity and brought to the Island of Hispaniola to be sold as slaves. When the Spaniards saw that some of these had escaped, they sent a ship to find them, and it voyaged for three years among the islands searching for those who had escaped being slaughtered, for a good Christian had helped them escape, taking pity on them and had won them over to Christ;[6] of these there were eleven persons and these I saw.

More than thirty other islands in the vicinity of San Juan are for the most part and for the same reason depopulated, and the land laid waste. On these islands I estimate there are 2,100 leagues of land that have been ruined and depopulated, empty of people.[7]

As for the vast mainland, which is ten times larger than all Spain, even including Aragon and Portugal, containing more land than the distance between Seville and Jerusalem, or more than two thousand leagues, we are sure that our Spaniards, with their cruel and abominable acts, have devastated the land and exterminated the rational people who fully inhabited it. We can estimate very surely and truthfully that in the forty years that have passed, with the infernal actions of the Christians, there have been unjustly slain more than <u>twelve million men, women, and children</u>. In truth, I believe without trying to deceive myself that the number of the slain is more like fifteen million.

The common ways mainly employed by the Spaniards who call themselves Christian and who have gone there to extirpate those pitiful nations and wipe them off the earth is by unjustly waging cruel and bloody wars. Then, when they have slain all those who fought for their lives or to escape the tortures they would have to endure, that is to say, when they have slain all the native rulers and young men (since the Spaniards usually spare only the women and children, who are subjected to the hardest and bitterest servitude ever suffered by man or beast), they enslave any survivors. With these infernal methods of tyranny they debase and weaken countless numbers of those pitiful Indian nations.

Their reason for killing and destroying such an infinite number of souls is that the Christians have an ultimate aim, which is to acquire gold, and to swell themselves with riches in a very brief time and thus rise to a high estate disproportionate to their merits. It should be kept in mind that their insatiable greed and ambition, the greatest ever seen in the world, is the cause of their villainies. And also, those lands are so rich and felicitous, the native peoples so meek and patient, so easy to subject, that our Spaniards have no more consideration for them than beasts. And I say this from my own knowledge of the acts I witnessed. But I should not say "than beasts" for, thanks be to God,

31

they have treated beasts with some respect; I should say instead like excrement on the public squares. And thus they have deprived the Indians of their lives and souls, for the millions I mentioned have died without the Faith and without the benefit of the sacraments. This is a well-known and proven fact which even the tyrant Governors, themselves killers, know and admit. And never have the Indians in all the Indies committed any act against the Spanish Christians, until those Christians have first and many times committed countless cruel aggressions against them or against neighboring nations. For in the beginning the Indians regarded the Spaniards as angels from Heaven.[8] Only after the Spaniards had used violence against them, killing, robbing, torturing, did the Indians ever rise up against them.

HISPANIOLA

On the Island Hispaniola was where the Spaniards first landed, as I have said. Here those Christians perpetrated their first ravages and oppressions against the native peoples. This was the first land in the New World to be destroyed and depopulated by the Christians, and here they began their subjection of the women and children, taking them away from the Indians to use them and ill use them, eating the food they provided with their sweat and toil. The Spaniards did not content themselves with what the Indians gave them of their own free will, according to their ability, which was always too little to satisfy enormous appetites, for a Christian eats and consumes in one day an amount of food that would suffice to feed three houses inhabited by ten Indians for one month. And they committed other <u>acts of force and violence and oppression</u> which made the Indians realize that these men had not come from Heaven. And some of the Indians concealed their foods while others concealed their wives and children and still others fled to the mountains to avoid the terrible transactions of the Christians.

And the Christians attacked them with buffets and beatings, until finally they laid hands on the nobles of the villages. Then they behaved with such temerity and shamelessness that the most powerful ruler of the islands had to see his own wife raped by a Christian officer.

From that time onward the Indians began to seek ways to throw the Christians out of their lands. They took up arms, <u>but their weapons were very weak and of little service in offense</u> and still less in defense. (Because of this, the wars of the Indians against each other are little more than games played by children.) And the Christians, with their horses and swords and pikes began to carry out massacres and strange cruelties against them. They attacked the towns and spared neither the children nor the aged nor pregnant women nor women in childbed, not only stabbing them and dismembering them but cutting them to pieces as if dealing with sheep in the slaughter house. They laid bets as to who, with one stroke of the sword, could split a man in two or could cut off his head or spill out his entrails with a single stroke of the pike. They took infants from their mothers' breasts, snatching them by the legs and pitching them headfirst against the crags or snatched them by the arms and threw them into the rivers, roaring with laughter and saying as the babies fell into the water, "Boil there, you offspring of the devil!" Other infants they put to the sword along with their mothers and anyone else who happened to be nearby. They made some low wide gallows on which the hanged victim's feet almost touched the ground, stringing up their victims in lots of thirteen, in memory of Our Redeemer and His twelve Apostles, then set burning wood at their feet and thus burned them alive. To others they attached straw or wrapped their whole bodies in straw and set them afire. With still others, all those they wanted to capture alive, they cut off their hands and hung them round the victim's neck, saying, "Go now, carry the message," meaning, Take the news to the Indians who have fled to the mountains. They usually dealt with the chieftains and nobles in the following way: they made a grid of rods which they placed on forked sticks, then lashed the victims to the grid and lighted a smoldering fire underneath, so that little by little, as those captives screamed in despair and torment, their souls would leave them.

I once saw this, when there were four or five nobles lashed on grids and burning; I seem even to recall that there were two or three pairs of grids where others were burning, and because they uttered such loud screams that they disturbed the captain's sleep, he ordered them to be strangled. And the constable, who was worse than an executioner, did not want to obey that order (and I know the name of that constable and know his relatives in Seville), but instead put a stick over the victims' tongues, so they could not make a sound, and he stirred up the fire, but not too much, so that they roasted slowly, as he liked. I saw all these things I have described, and countless others.

And because all the people who could do so fled to the mountains to escape these inhuman, ruthless, and ferocious acts, the Spanish captains, enemies of the human race, pursued them with the fierce dogs[9] they kept which attacked the Indians, tearing them to pieces and devouring them. And because on few and far between occasions, the Indians justifiably killed some Christians, the Spaniards made a rule among themselves that for every Christian slain by the Indians, they would slay a hundred Indians.

THE KINGDOMS THAT ONCE EXISTED ON THE ISLAND HISPANIOLA

On the island Hispaniola there were five very large principalities ruled by five very powerful Kings to whom almost all the other rulers paid tribute, since there were other princes in distant provinces who recognized no one as their superior. There was a kingdom called Maguá, the last syllable accented, which name means "The Realm of the Fertile Lowlands." This land is among the most notable and admirable places in the world, for it stretches across the island from the southern sea to the northern sea, a distance of eighty leagues. It averages five leagues in width but at times is eight to ten and is of very high altitude from one part to another and is drained by more than thirty thousand rivers and creeks, twelve of the rivers being as large as the Ebro and Duero and Guadalquivir combined. All the rivers flow from the western highland, which means that twenty or twenty-five thousand of them are rich in gold. For in those highlands lies the province of Cibao, where are the famous Cibao mines harboring a fine and remarkable pure gold.

The King who ruled this realm was called Guarionex. Great lords were his vassals, one of them having assembled an army of sixteen thousand men to serve Guarionex, and I know or knew some of them. That virtuous King Guarionex was by nature very pacific and was devotedly obedient to the Kings of Castile and in certain years gave them, through the nobles under his command, a generous amount of gold dust. Each man who had a house was given for this purpose a spherical bell, or rather, a spherical grain measure resembling a bell. This was stuffed full with gold dust (brought down by the rivers) for the people of this realm did not have the skill to work the mines. When there was not enough, some years, to fill the measure, then it was cut in half and one half was filled. This King Guarionex proclaimed himself ready to serve the King of Castile with a labor force that would be brought to Santo Domingo from the city of Isabella, the first Christian settlement, fifty leagues distant, and said, with reason, that they should not have to pay in gold because his vassals did not know how to procure it. That labor force, he said, would work the mines with great heartiness and their labor would be worth to the King of Spain, each year, more than three million castellanos.[10] And had that labor force been so employed, there would be, today, more than fifty cities the size of Seville, on this island.

The recompense they gave this great and good Indian

ruler was to dishonor him through his wife, who was raped by a Christian officer. And King Guarionex, who, in time, could have assembled his people to avenge him, chose instead to go alone into hiding and die exiled from his kingdom, deprived of his rank and possessions, placing himself under the protection of the chieftain of the province called Ciguayos, one of his vassals.

When his hiding place was discovered, the Christians waged war on Ciguayos, massacring a great number of people until they finally took the exiled King and, in chains, put him on a vessel that was to take him to Castile. But the vessel was lost at sea and with it were drowned many Christians along with the captive King, and in this shipwreck was lost a quantity of gold dust and gold nuggets weighing the equivalent of 3,600 castellanos. Such was God's vengeance for so many terrible injustices.

Another kingdom on the island was called Marién and is now called Puerto Real. It is situated at the end of the fertile lowlands toward the north and is larger than Portugal, although much more suitable for development and settlement. Many mountain chains exist here, which are rich in copper and gold. The King of this province was called Guacanagarí, many of whose vassals were known to me. It was this King who welcomed the Admiral[11] when he first landed in the New World and set foot on the island of Hispaniola.

The welcome extended by this King to the Admiral and all those accompanying him could not have been more cordial and generous, even had it been the voyagers' native land and their own King greeting them with food and provisions of every kind, everything that was needed, which was a great deal, for the vessel on which Columbus had voyaged was lost here.

I know all this from conversations with the Admiral.

Well, that same King, while fleeing to the mountains to escape the cruel persecutions meted out to him and his people by the Christians, died, having been stripped of his rank and possessions by those same Christians, and all his vassals perished in the tyrannical persecutions and enslavements which I shall later on describe.

The third kingdom on the island of Hispaniola was Maguana, where the best sugar in that island is now made. The King of that realm was called Caonabó and in condition and importance he surpassed all the others. The Spaniards captured this unhappy King by using great and wicked subtlety, laying hands on him while he was in his house. Afterward, they put him on a ship outward bound for Castile. But while still in port with six other outward-bound vessels, God desired to manifest Himself against this great iniquity and sent a violent storm that sank all the vessels and drowned all the Christians on board, along with the shackled King of Maguana.

This native ruler had three or four brothers, who, like him, were strong and fearless. When their brother and lord was taken captive and his subjects killed or enslaved, these brothers, upon seeing the slaughter being carried out by the Christians, took up arms in revenge. The Christians met their attack with cavalry (horses being the most pernicious weapon against the Indians) and in the battles that followed half the land was laid waste and depopulated.

The fourth kingdom was that of Xaraguá and it was like the marrow and medulla of the island, its sovereign court. Its King surpassed all the other princes in eloquence, refinement, and education and good breeding. Likewise, his government was the best ordered and the most circumspect. At his court there was a multitude of nobles whose beauty and elegance excelled all others.

Behechio, the King of Xaraguá, had a sister, by name Anacaona. Together, the brother and sister rendered great services to the Kings of Castile and afforded great benefactions to the Christians, helping them to avoid countless mortal dangers. After the death of her brother the King, Anacaona continued to rule the land.

Then, one day the Christian Governor[12] of the island arrived with a cavalry force of sixty horses and three hundred foot soldiers. The cavalry alone could lay waste the land. Having been promised safe conduct there soon arrived three hundred Indian nobles. These, or most of them, were tricked into entering a very big Indian house of straw where they were shut in and burned alive when the house was set on fire. Those who did not perish in the conflagration were put to the sword or the pike, along with a countless number of the common people. As a special honor, the lady Anacaona was hanged.

And it happened that those Christians, either out of piety or cupidity, took some boys to shield them from the slaughter and placed them on the croup of their horses. But other Spaniards came up from behind and ran the boys through with their pikes. When the victims fell from the horses the Spaniards cut off their legs with a sword.

Some of the nobles who managed to flee from this inhuman cruelty took refuge on a small island nearby, about eight leagues out to sea. And the said Christian Governor condemned all those who had gone there to be sold as slaves because they had fled the butchery.

The fifth kingdom was called Higüey and its ruler was an aged queen who was called Higuanamá. They hanged her. And there were countless people that I saw burned alive or cut to pieces or tortured in many new ways of killing and inflicting pain. They also made slaves of many Indians.

Because the particulars that enter into these outrages are so numerous they could not be contained in the scope of much writing, for in truth I believe that in the great deal I have set down here I have not revealed the thousandth part of the sufferings endured by the Indians, I now want only to add that, in the matter of these unprovoked and destructive wars, and God is my witness, all these acts of wickedness I have described, as well as those I have omitted, were perpetrated against the Indians without cause, without any more cause than could give a community of good monks living together in a monastery. And still more strongly I affirm that until the multitude of people on this island of Hispaniola were killed and their lands devastated, they committed no sin against the Christians that would be punishable by man's laws, and as to those sins punishable by God's law, such as vengeful feelings against such powerful enemies as the Christians have been, those sins would be committed by the very few Indians who are hardhearted and impetuous. And I can say this from my great experience with them: their hardness and impetuosity would be that of children, of boys ten or twelve years old. I know by certain infallible signs that the wars waged by the Indians against the Christians have been justifiable wars and that all the wars waged by the Christians against the Indians have been unjust wars, more diabolical than any wars ever waged anywhere in the world. This I declare to be so of all the many wars they have waged against the peoples throughout the Indies.

After the wars and the killings had ended, when usually there survived only some boys, some women, and children, these survivors were distributed among the Christians to be slaves. The *repartimiento* or distribution was made according to the rank and importance of the Christian to whom the Indians were allocated, one of them being given thirty, another forty, still another, one or two hundred, and besides the rank of the Christian there was also to be considered in what favor he stood with the tyrant they called Governor. The pretext was that these allocated Indians were to be instructed in the articles of the Christian Faith. As if those Christians who were as a rule foolish and cruel and greedy and vicious could be caretakers of souls! And the care they took was to send the men to the mines to dig for gold, which is intolerable labor, and to send the women into the fields of the big ranches to hoe and till the land, work suitable for strong men. Nor to either the men or the women did they give any food except herbs and legumes, things of little substance. The milk in the breasts of the women with infants dried up and thus in a short while the infants perished.

repartamiento

made natives labor

babies died, moms - no milk

41

And since men and women were separated, there could be no marital relations. And the men died in the mines and the women died on the ranches from the same causes, exhaustion and hunger. And thus was depopulated that island which had been densely populated.

I will speak only briefly of the heavy loads the Indians were made to carry, loads weighing three to four arrobas,[13] Christian tyrants and captains had themselves carried in hammocks borne by two Indians. This shows that they treated the Indians as beasts of burden. But were I to describe all this and the buffetings and beatings and birchings endured by the Indians at their labors, no amount of time and paper could encompass this task.

And be it noted that the worst depredations on these islands in the New World began when tidings came of the death of Her most Serene Highness, Queen Isabel, which occurred in the year one thousand five hundred and four. Because, up to that time, only a few provinces on the island of Hispaniola had been destroyed in unjust wars, but not the entire island, since, for the most part, the island was under the royal protection of the Queen and she, may God rest her, took admirable and zealous care of these people, their salvation and prosperity, as we saw with our own eyes and touched with our hands.

Another rule should be noted: in all parts of the Indies, wherever they have landed or passed through, the Christians have always committed atrocities against the Indians, have perpetrated the slaughters and tyrannies and abominable oppressions against innocent people that we have described, and have added worse and more cruel

42

acts, ever since God allowed them most suddenly to fall into dishonor and opprobrium.

THE ISLANDS OF SAN JUAN AND JAMAICA

The Spaniards passed over to the islands of San Juan and Jamaica (both of them veritable gardens and beehives of activity) in the year one thousand five hundred and nine, with the aim and purpose of making these islands a part of Hispaniola.

And on those islands the Spaniards perpetrated the same acts of aggression against the Indians and the wicked deeds described above, adding to them many outstanding cruelties, massacres and burnings of the people, or executing them by flinging them to the fierce dogs, torturing and oppressing the survivors, condemning them to the hard labor of the mines, thus eradicating them from the earth, despoiling the land of those unfortunate and innocent people. Before the arrival of the Spaniards there had lived on these islands more than six hundred thousand souls, it has been stated. I believe there were more than one million inhabitants, and now, in each of the two islands, there are no more than two hundred persons, all the others having perished without the Faith and without the holy sacraments.

THE ISLAND OF CUBA

In the year one thousand five hundred and eleven, the Spaniards passed over to the island of Cuba, which as I have said is at the same distance from Hispaniola as the distance between Valladolid and Rome, and which was a

well-populated province. They began and ended in Cuba
as they had done elsewhere, but with much greater acts of
cruelty.

Among the noteworthy outrages they committed was
the one they perpetrated against a cacique, a very important noble, by name Hatuey, who had come to Cuba from
Hispaniola with many of his people, to flee the calamities
and inhuman acts of the Christians. When he was told by
certain Indians that the Christians were now coming to
Cuba, he assembled as many of his followers as he could
and said this to them: "Now you must know that they are
saying the Christians are coming here, and you know by
experience how they have put So and So and So and So,
and other nobles to an end. And now they are coming
from Haiti (which is Hispaniola) to do the same here. Do
you know why they do this?" The Indians replied: "We
do not know. But it may be that they are by nature wicked
and cruel." And he told them: "No, they do not act only
because of that, but because they have a God they greatly
worship and they want us to worship that God, and that
is why they struggle with us and subject us and kill us."

He had a basket full of gold and jewels and he said:
"You see their God here, the God of the Christians. If you
agree to it, let us dance for this God, who knows, it may
please the God of the Christians and then they will do us
no harm." And his followers said, all together, "Yes, that
is good, that is good!" And they danced round the basket
of gold until they fell down exhausted. Then their chief,
the cacique Hatuey, said to them: "See here, if we keep
this basket of gold they will take it from us and will end

up by killing us. So let us cast away the basket into the river." They all agreed to do this, and they flung the basket of gold into the river that was nearby.

This cacique, Hatuey, was constantly fleeing before the Christians from the time they arrived on the island of Cuba, since he knew them and of what they were capable. Now and then they encountered him and he defended himself, but they finally killed him. And they did this for the sole reason that he had fled from those cruel and wicked Christians and had defended himself against them. And when they had captured him and as many of his followers as they could, they burned them all at the stake.

When tied to the stake, the cacique Hatuey was told by a Franciscan friar who was present, an artless rascal, something about the God of the Christians and of the articles of the Faith. And he was told what he could do in the brief time that remained to him, in order to be saved and go to Heaven. The cacique, who had never heard any of this before, and was told he would go to Inferno where, if he did not adopt the Christian Faith, he would suffer eternal torment, asked the Franciscan friar if Christians all went to Heaven. When told that they did he said he would prefer to go to Hell. Such is the fame and honor that God and our Faith have earned through the Christians who have gone out to the Indies.

On one occasion when we went to claim ten leagues of a big settlement, along with food and maintenance, we were welcomed with a bounteous quantity of fish and bread and cooked victuals. The Indians generously gave us all they could. Then suddenly, without cause and without warning, and in my presence, the devil inhabited the Christians and spurred them to attack the Indians, men, women, and children, who were sitting there before us. In the massacre that followed, the Spaniards put to the sword more than three thousand souls. I saw such terrible cruelties done there as I had never seen before nor thought to see.

A few days later, knowing that news of this massacre had spread through the land, I sent messengers ahead to the chiefs of the province of Havana, knowing they had heard good things about me, telling them we were about to visit the town and telling them they should not hide but should come out to meet us, assuring them that no harm would be done to them. I did this with the full knowledge of the captain.[14] And when we arrived in the province, there came out to welcome us twenty-one chiefs and caciques, and our captain, breaking his pledge to me and the pledge I had made to them, took all these chieftains captive, intending to burn them at the stake, telling me this would be a good thing because those chiefs had in the past done him some harm. I had great difficulty in saving those Indians from the fire, but finally succeeded.

Afterward, when all the Indians of this island were subjected to servitude and the same ruin had befallen there as on the island Hispaniola, the survivors began to flee to the mountains or in despair to hang themselves, and there were husbands and wives who hanged themselves together with their children, because the cruelties perpetrated by one very great Spaniard[15] (whom I knew) were so horrifying. More than two hundred Indians hanged themselves.

And thus perished a countless number of people on the island of Cuba.

That tyrant Spaniard, representative of the King of Spain, demanded, in the *repartimiento,* that he be given three hundred Indians. At the end of three months all but thirty of them had died of the hard labor in the mines, which is to say only a tenth of them had survived. He demanded another allocation of Indians, and they also perished in the same way. He demanded still another large allocation, and those Indians also perished. Then he died, and the devil bore him away.

In three or four months, when I was there, more than seventy thousand children, whose fathers and mothers had been sent to the mines, died of hunger.

And I saw other frightful things. The Spaniards finally decided to track down the Indians who had taken refuge in the mountains. There they created amazing havoc and thus finished ravaging the island. Where had been a flourishing population, it is now a shame and pity to see the island laid waste and turned into a desert.

THE MAINLAND

In the year one thousand five hundred and fourteen there went to the mainland a wretch of a Governor,[16] a most cruel tyrant, ruthless and imprudent, lacking any piety. He regarded himself as an instrument of Divine Wrath. His chief aim was to settle the mainland with a large population of Spaniards. Other tyrants had gone to the mainland before him, and had robbed and committed many atrocities along the coast, but now this Governor surpassed all others who had ravaged the mainland in the cruelties he committed. His nefarious deeds went far beyond past abominations in the Indies. He ruthlessly exterminated the people and turned the land into an inferno. He laid waste the land for many leagues between Darién[17] and the southern kingdom of Nicaragua, that is to say, more than five hundred leagues of what had been the richest and most densely populated locality in the New World. Many great chieftains had ruled it, for this land possessed a wealth of gold such as had not been seen by the Spaniards, even on the island of Hispaniola where large quantities of gold had been extracted from the bowels of the earth by the Indians (who died of that hard labor) with which Spain has been stuffed.

This tyrant-Governor who had gone to the mainland along with a large company of Spaniards invented new cruelties, new methods of torture to force the Indians to reveal and hand over their stores of gold. One captain, at the orders of the Governor, slew in a single attack more than forty thousand Indians. This massacre was witnessed by a Franciscan religious who was with him, by name Fray Francisco de San Román. The people were killed by the sword, by fire, by being torn to pieces by the fierce dogs kept by the Spaniards, and by being tortured to death in various ways.

And because of the pernicious blindness that has always afflicted those who have ruled in the Indies, nothing was done to *incline* the Indians to embrace the one true Faith, they were rounded up and in large numbers *forced* to do so. Inasmuch as the conversion of the Indians to Chris-

48

tianity was stated to be the principal aim of the Spanish conquerors, they have dissimulated the fact that only with blood and fire have the Indians been brought to embrace the Faith and to swear obedience to the kings of Castile, or by threats of being slain or taken into captivity. As if the Son of God who died for each one of them would have countenanced such a thing! For He commanded His Apostles: "Go ye to all the people" *(Euntes docete omnes gentes).* Christ Jesus would have made no such demands of these peaceable infidels who cultivate the soil of their native lands. Yet they are told they must embrace the Christian Faith immediately, without hearing any sermon preached and without any indoctrination. They are told to subject themselves to a King they have never heard of nor seen and are told this by the King's messengers who are such despicable and cruel tyrants that deprive them of their liberty, their possessions, their wives and children. This is not only absurd but worthy of scorn.

This wretch of a Governor thus gave such instructions in order to justify his and their presence in the Indies, they themselves being absurd, irrational, and unjust when he sent the thieves under his command to attack and rob a settlement of Indians where he had heard there was a store of gold, telling them to go at night when the inhabitants were securely in their houses and that, when half a league away from the settlement, they should read in a loud voice his order: "Caciques and Indians of this land, hark ye! We notify you that there is but one God and one Pope and one King of Castile who is the lord of these lands. Give heed and show obedience!" Etcetera, etcetera. "And if not, be warned that we will wage war against you and will slay you or take you into captivity." Etc., etc.

Then, in the early dawn, when these innocents are asleep with their wives and children, the Spaniards attack and enter the town and set fire to the houses, which, being commonly made of straw, burn rapidly with all who are within them.

Thus they proceeded, killing as many as they liked, and torturing those they took alive, because they had been told of other settlements where there was gold, more than there was in this one, and then they took a number of survivors in chains to sell them as slaves.

They always searched for gold in the ruins of the towns they burned. In this manner and with such acts, that Godforsaken Governor busied himself and his company from the year fourteen until the year twenty-one or twenty-two, sending into those actions five or six of his officers, giving each of them such and such an amount of the booty. The major part of the gold, the pearls, the en-slaved Indians falling to himself as their captain–general. The representatives of the King acted in the same way, each one sending out as many underlings as they could, and the first Bishop of that kingdom also sent out his underlings so as to have his share of the treasure-trove. I believe I underestimate when I say they robbed more gold in that time and in that kingdom than was worth one million castellanos, of which amount they sent to the King only three thousand castellanos. And during these actions they killed some eight hundred thousand souls.

The other tyrant who succeeded this one on the mainland until the year one thousand five hundred and twenty-three, killed and allowed to be killed by his henchmen in the wars that followed all the native peoples that survived.

That wretch of a Governor who first penetrated the mainland committed countless vile deeds, of which I shall mention a few. A cacique (as a native ruler was called) had given the tyrant, either of his own accord or impelled by fear, gold worth nine thousand castellanos. Not content with this amount, the Governor had the cacique bound to a stake in a sitting posture, his legs extended, and set a fire to burn the soles of his feet, demanding more gold. The cacique sent to his house for more gold and the servant brought back three thousand castellanos' worth. Not content with this, more gold was demanded of the cacique. And, either because there was no more or else he was unwilling to give more, he continued to be tortured until the bone marrow came out of the soles of his feet and he died. Such things were done to the Indians countless times, always with the aim of getting as much gold as possible from them.

Another instance of such cruelty was when a company of Spaniards made an attack on a mountain refuge where some Indians were hiding from the pestilential acts of the Christians. Falling upon this numerous band, the Spaniards captured some women and maidens, sixty or eighty of them, holding them captive while they killed most of the men. Next day, some of the surviving Indians, anxious about the captive women, came upon the Christians from the rear and attacked them. Seeing they were hard-pressed, the Christians, who hesitated to bring up their cavalry, set their swords against the bodies of the women and maids, leaving not one of them alive. At sight of this, the Indians screamed in an access of grief and horror: "Oh, vile men! Oh, cruel Christians! So you kill women? (In their language their word for women is *iras,* meaning wrath, or vengeance.)

At a distance of ten or fifteen leagues from Panama was a great chief named Paris, who was very rich in gold. The Spaniards went there and he received them as if they were brothers, presenting the captain with gold worth fifty thousand castellanos, giving this of his own free will. It seemed to the captain of the Christian troops that anyone who could give that amount freely must possess a very great quantity (and discovering such treasures of gold was their sole aim and consolation). They dissimulated and made as if to depart. But in the early dawn they turned back and fell upon the town, setting fire to it, killing and burning many people. When the fires died down, they found and took away gold worth fifty or sixty thousand castellanos.

The cacique managed to escape, was neither killed nor captured, and very quickly he assembled as many surviving Indians as he could, and by the end of two or three days caught up with the Christians who were carrying away his gold, and valiantly attacked them, killing fifty Christians and taking the gold from them. The others, badly wounded, fled. But later on they marched against that cacique with a large company and killed him, along with a great many of his troops, taking captives and subjecting them to slavery in the usual way. In short, at the present time there remains no vestige of the large town where once ruled a great chieftain. And this does not take into account the killings and destructions that wretch of a Governor carried out which resulted in the extinction of those kingdoms.

THE PROVINCE OF NICARAGUA

In the year one thousand five hundred and twenty-three, at the end of the year, this same tyrant went into Nicaragua to subjugate that most flourishing province and a sorrowful hour it was when he entered that land. Who could exaggerate the felicity, the good health, the amenities of that prosperous and numerous population? Verily it was a joy to behold that admirable province with its big towns, some of them extending three or four leagues, full of gardens and orchards and prosperous people. But because this land is a great plain without any mountains where the people could take refuge, they had to allow, with great anguish, the Christians to remain in the province and to suffer cruel persecutions from them. And since these Indians were by nature very gentle and peace-loving, the tyrant and his comrades (all of whom had aided him in destroying other kingdoms) inflicted such damage, carried out such slaughters, took so many captives, perpetrated so many unjust acts that no human tongue could describe them.

He once sent fifty horsemen with pikes to destroy an entire province. Not a single human being survived that massacre, neither women nor children nor aged and infirm. And that province was larger than the county of

Rusellón in Spain. This terrible massacre was punishment for a trifling offense: some Indians had not responded to a summons promptly enough when the tyrant had commanded that they bring him a load of maize (that grain taking the place of wheat in this region), or else had asked for more Indians to be assigned to serve him or his comrades. And there was no place where the Indians could take refuge from the tyrant–Governor's wrath.

He sent companies of Spaniards to open up other provinces—that is to say, to attack and pillage the peoples in those provinces. They were allowed to capture as many Indians as they liked in peaceful settlements, to become their slaves. And they put the captives in chains and made them carry heavy loads, weighing as much as three arrobas. And they had to carry these cargoes on their backs for long marches. The result was that the number of captives soon dwindled, most of them dying from exhaustion, so that from four thousand captives there remained only six. They left the dead bodies on the trail. They were decapitated corpses, for when a captive sank under the heavy load, the Spaniards cut off his head, which fell to one side while the body fell to the other while the captives chained together continued their march without interruption. When commanded to do similar labor, with this experience behind them, the surviving Indians went off weeping and saying, "These are the roads down which we went to serve the Christians. In the past, even when we worked hard we could return to our houses, our wives, and children. But now we go without hope of ever again seeing them."

This tyrant once took it into his head to make a new *repartimiento* (distribution of captives among the Spaniards) this being either a caprice of his or, as was rumored, to rid himself of some Indians he disliked and pass them on to someone else. This occurred at the time of year when grain should be sowed and it kept the Indians from their usual tasks at seed-time. Later on, as a result, the Christians lacked grain, whereupon they seized the stores of grain the Indians kept for themselves and their families. In the famine that followed, more than thirty thousand Indians perished of starvation and there were cases when a woman would kill and eat her own child, in desperation.

Since all the settlements of the Indians in this fertile land were situated in the midst of gardens and orchards, the Christians resided in them, each Christian taking over the houses of the Indians who had been allocated to him according to the royal grant known as the *encomienda*. The Indian who had owned the house now worked for the Christian as his servant, cooking his meals, tilling the soil, working without rest. Oh, the pitiful Indians! Men and women, the aged and the children all worked for this Spanish Christian. For the children, as soon as they could stand on their legs, were put to work. And thus the Indians have been used up and consumed, and the few who survive are still being wasted away. Nor are these hard-working Indians allowed to own a house or anything of their own, and in this respect the Spaniards in Nicaragua have gone beyond the excesses of injustice that have prevailed on the island of Hispaniola.

The greatest and most horrible pestilence that has laid

waste the province of Nicaragua was the freedom given by the Governor to his subordinates in the matter of petitioning slaves from the caciques of the towns. They petitioned every four or five months and each time a new allotment. The Governor could obtain fifty slaves at a time by threatening the cacique with being burned at the stake or thrown to the fierce dogs if he refused. Since the Indians do not commonly have slaves, at the most a cacique may have two or three or four, he simply went through the settlement, taking to begin with all the orphans, then taking one son from those who had two, and two sons from those who had three. In this way the cacique completed the number demanded by the tyrant, with loud lamentations and weeping by the people, for it seems they most greatly love their sons. And since this act was repeated many times, that whole kingdom became depopulated during the twenties and until the year thirty-three.

For this transaction was aided by six or seven ships voyaging along the coast to take on board and sell the surplus requisitioned slaves in Panama and Peru. And all of those captives soon died for as it has been ascertained from experience repeated a thousand times, the Indians when uprooted from their native land very soon perish. Then, too, they are never given enough to eat and their labor is never lightened in any way, since they are bought and sold to do only heavy work.

Thus more than five hundred thousand Indians were torn out of this province and sold into slavery. And those Indians had been as free as I am. In the infernal wars waged by the Spaniards another five or six hundred thousand souls have perished up to the present time. And these ravages continue. In a matter of fourteen years this province has undergone these things. There must now be in Nicaragua four or five thousand Spaniards who kill, each day, through acts of violence, oppression, and servitude, numerous Indians, and they boast that they have established one of the great population centers in the world.

NEW SPAIN

In the year one thousand five hundred and seven New Spain[18] was discovered and during the discovery great outrages were perpetrated against the Indians and some of the discoverers were slain. In the year one thousand five hundred and eighteen, Spaniards who called themselves Christians went there to massacre and kill, although they said their aim was to settle Christians in the province. And from that year to this day (we are in the year one thousand five hundred and forty-two), the climax of injustice and violence and tyranny committed against the Indians has been reached and surpassed. Because the Spaniards have now lost all fear of God and of the King, they have ceased to know right from wrong. Because among so many and such different nations they have committed and continue to commit so many acts of cruelty, such terrible ravages, massacres, destructions, exterminations, thefts, violences and tyrannies of all kinds that all the things we have related are as nothing by comparison. But were we to describe all the infinite number of such acts they would be as nothing when compared to what they have done this day and year of one thousand five hundred and forty-two, and today in this month of September are doing, for they continue to commit acts of the most abominable kind. As we have said above, the rule is always this: from the beginning the Spaniards have always continually increased and expanded their infernal acts and outrages.

Thus, from the beginning of their discovery of New Spain, that is to say, from the eighteenth of April in the year one thousand five hundred and eighteen until the year thirty, a period of twelve whole years, there were continual massacres and outrages committed by the bloody hands and swords of the Spaniards against the Indians living on the four hundred and fifty leagues of land surrounding the city of Mexico, which comprised four or five great kingdoms as large as and more felicitous than Spain. Those lands were all more densely populated than Toledo or Seville and Valladolid and Zaragoza all combined, along with Barcelona. Never has there been such a population as in these cities which God saw fit to place in that vast expanse of land having a circumference of more than a thousand leagues. The Spaniards have killed more Indians here in twelve years by the sword, by fire, and enslavement than anywhere else in the Indies. They have killed young and old, men, women, and children,[19] some four million souls during what they call the Conquests, which were the violent invasions of cruel tyrants that should be condemned not only by the law of God but by all the laws of man (since they were much worse than the deeds committed by the Turks in their effort to destroy the Christian Church). And this does not take into account those Indians who have died from ill treatment or were killed under tyrannical servitude.

In particulars, no tongue would suffice, nor word nor human efforts, to narrate the frightful deeds committed simultaneously by the Spaniards in regions far distant from each other, those notorious hellions, enemies of humankind. And some of their deeds committed in the Indies, in their quality and circumstances, truly they could not, even with much time and diligence and writing, could not be explained. I will narrate, along with protests and sworn statements by eyewitnesses, only some portions of the story, for I could not hope to explain a thousandth part.

Among other massacres there was the one in a big city of more than thirty thousand inhabitants, which is called Cholula. The people came out to welcome all the lords of the country and the earth; first of all came the priests with the head priest of the Christians in procession and received them with great respect and reverence, and took them to lodge in the center of the town, where they would reside in the houses of the most important nobles.

Soon after this the Spaniards agreed to carry out a massacre, or as they called it a punitive attack, in order to sow terror and apprehension, and to make a display of their power in every corner of that land. This was always the determination of the Spaniards in all the lands they conquered: to commit a great massacre that would terrorize the tame flock and make it tremble.

With this aim, therefore, they sent a summons to all the caciques and nobles of the city and in the localities subject to it, and also the head chieftain, and as they arrived to speak with the Spanish captain they were taken prisoner, so unexpectedly that none could flee and warn the others.

The Spaniards had asked for five or six thousand Indians to carry their cargo. When all the chiefs had come, they and the burden-bearers were herded into the patios of the houses. What a grievous thing it was, to see those Indians as they prepared to carry the loads of the Spaniards: it was a grievous sight for they came naked, stark naked except for their private parts, which were covered. And they had a netting bag slung over their shoulders, holding their meager nourishment. They were all made to squat down on their haunches like tame sheep.

When they were all placed close together they were bound and tied. At the closed doorways armed guards took turns to see that none escaped. Then, at a command, all the Spaniards drew their swords or pikes and while their chiefs looked on, helpless, all those tame sheep were butchered, cut to pieces. At the end of two or three days some survivors came out from under the corpses, wounded but still alive, and they went, weeping, to the Spaniards, imploring mercy, which was denied. The Spaniards had no compassion but drove them back and cut them down. Then the Spaniards had the chiefs, a total of more than a hundred, who were already shackled, burned at the stakes that had been driven into the ground.

But one of the caciques, and who knows, he may have been the ruler of that land, managed to escape with twenty or thirty of his followers. They took refuge in the great temple that was there, which was like a fortress, and was called *Cuu,* and there he defended himself for the greater part of the day. But the Spaniards, against whom there is no protection, especially no protection for these unarmed people, set fire to the temple and burned them there as they cried out: "Oh, wicked men! What have we done against you? Why are you killing us? Go to the city of Mexico, where our lord and master, Montezuma, will revenge us!"

It is said that when the Spaniards were putting the five or six thousand Indians in the patios to the sword one captain sang out: "Nero of Tarpeia watched Rome burn and the cries of the young and the old did not move him."

They carried out another great massacre in the city of Tepeaca, which was much larger and more densely populated than Cholula. Many perished, too many to count, and great acts of particular cruelty were committed.

From Cholula they marched toward the city of Mexico, and the great Montezuma sent them thousands of presents and an assembly of chiefs and people celebrated fiestas on the road, and as the Spaniards reached the pavements of the city at a distance of two leagues, the great ruler sent them his own brother accompanied by many nobles, bearing gifts of silver and gold and rich garments. At the entrance to the city he himself greeted them and accompanied them to the palace in which he had arranged for them to be lodged. And that very day, as I was told by some of those who were there, the Spaniards deceitfully set a guard of eighty men to capture the great King Montezuma and put him in chains.

But I leave all this, even though there are many important events to relate, and shall only summarize what those tyrants did. The captain–general took his troops down to the sea to encounter and defeat a certain other Spanish captain[20] who was marching against him, but left a number of his officers in Mexico City and about a hundred men to guard the captive King and gave them permission to commit an outstanding crime, with the aim of increasing and spreading terror throughout the land, using their utmost methods of cruelty.

The Indians, nobles and commoners alike, throughout the city, thinking only of giving pleasure to their lord imprisoned within the palace assembled nearby to celebrate a fiesta[21] in a public square, singing and dancing the dance they called *mitote* which is like the *arieta* of the islands. At this fiesta the nobles donned their gala costumes to display their wealth, and some of these nobles were of royal lineage. Celebrating this fiesta were more than a thousand nobles, the flower of Indian youth, the elite of Montezuma's empire.

The Spanish captain set out toward this fiesta with a company of his men and sent out other squadrons to the other fiestas being celebrated in other parts of the city, with orders that at a certain set time they were to attack the celebrants mercilessly, after pretending at first merely to be enjoying the fiestas.

Being a little drunk and having safely penetrated to the very center of the fiesta nearest the palace, he called out, "Now, Santiago be with us, and at them!" And with naked swords they attacked those delicate bodies, letting that generous blood flow, leaving not one of the Indian nobles to survive. While in other parts of the city the same atrocities were committed.

This was an event that spread terror throughout those

kingdoms and filled the people with bitterness, anguish, and revolt. That calamity, which deprived them of the flower of the nobility, meant, for them, the end of the world, and they have never ceased lamenting and recounting the story in their songs and the dances called *arietas,* as in their stories called "romances." They have never recovered from that loss of succession to all the nobility, which had been for many years their glory.

The unheard-of cruelty and injustice of this massacre stirred up the Indians to revolt, although until that time they had tolerated the imprisonment of their universal ruler, because Montezuma himself had commanded them not to plot against the Spanish conquerors. Now, throughout the city they took up arms, attacked the Christians, wounding and killing many of those who did not manage to escape. And when Montezuma came out into the corridors of the palace and commanded the Indians to go away in peace, their leader set his dagger against the King's breast and they all swore henceforth not to obey him and that they would consult together and elect another lord who would guide them in their battles.

For they intended to wage war against the captain–general when he should return from Veracruz, victorious. But when he did return, it was with a larger army of Christians, and the Indian uprising, which had lasted three or four days, was coming to an end.

The attack made by the augmented army against all the Indians of that land produced a battle so fierce that, fearing all the Christians would be slain, in self-defense they declared a truce and left the city. The Indians had killed a great many Christians on the bridges of the lagoon, in this righteous war.

After this, there followed the battle for the city, the Christians having returned in full strength and they created great havoc. In this strange and admirable kingdom of the Indies, they slew a countless number of people and burned alive many great chiefs.

Later, when the Spaniards had inflicted extraordinary abominations on the city of Mexico and the other cities and towns, over a surface of fifteen or twenty leagues, killing countless Indians, they pressed forward to spread terror and lay waste the province of Pánuco, where an amazing number of people were slain.

Likewise, they destroyed the province of Tututepec, and then the province of Ipilcingo, and after that the province of Colima, each of those lands being more vast than the kingdoms of León and Castile.[22] To recount the ravages and massacres and cruelties they perpetrated in each of those lands would no doubt be difficult if not impossible and would be a story unbearable to hear.

At this point we should take note of the reason the Spaniards gave for conquering these lands and why they tried to destroy all those innocents and to devastate those regions where the aspect of the joy and happiness of a numerous population should have caused them to become veritable Christians. Their aim, they said, was to subject the people to the King of Spain, who had commanded them to kill and to enslave. And the Indians who did not obey stupid messages and would not put themselves in the hands of the iniquitous and ruthless Christians would be

considered rebels unwilling to serve His Majesty. And
their argument was set down in letters addressed to our
lord the King. And the blindness of those who ruled the
Indies prevented them from understanding that in the
King's laws is expressed the following: that no one is or
can be called a rebel if, to begin with, he is not a subject
of the King. The Christians (who know something of God
and of reason and of human laws) should realize how
astounding all this is to simple people, living peacefully on
their lands and who have their own chiefs, to be told by
the Spaniards of a new Spanish ruler never seen or heard
of before, and that if they do not subject themselves to that
King they will be cut to pieces. It makes their hearts stand
still, for they have seen from experience that this will be
done. And the most horrifying thing is that the Indians
who do obey are placed in servitude where with incredible
hard labor and torments even harder to endure and longer
lasting than the torments of those who are put to the
sword they are finally, with their wives and children and
their entire generation exterminated. And now that, with
these fears and under threats, these peoples and others in
the New World have come to obey and to recognize the
authority of the foreign King, these rotten and inconstant
Viceroys, blinded and confused by ambition and diabolical
greed, do not see that they have not acquired one jot of
right as veritable representatives of the King, that both
natural and human and divine right are something quite
different, that they have acquired nothing when the Indians are terrorized into giving submission and tribute to the
foreign King but have earned the punishment of the devil

and of the eternal fires of hell. They do not see that they are even committing offenses against the King of Castile in destroying these kingdoms and in annihilating the inhabitants. Yet such are the services the Spaniards in the Indies have rendered to their King and are still rendering today.

It was with this supposedly just cause that the tyrant-Governors sent out two other tyrants[23] even more cruel and ferocious, of even less piety and mercy, to several flourishing and happy kingdoms. One of them went to Guatemala toward the southern sea, while the other proceeded to Naco and its bordering kingdoms of Honduras and Guaimura on the northern sea, which are, at a distance of three hundred leagues from Mexico. One of the captains went by land, the other by sea, each captain in command of many horsemen and foot soldiers.

I am stating the truth when I say that both captains committed wrongs, most notably the one who went to Guatemala, for the other one came to a bad end before he could commit so many ferocious deeds. But the injustices, cruelties, exterminations committed in Guatemala comprise a story that horrifies the centuries, past, present, and to come, and these alone would swell a very big book. Because the campaign of that captain surpassed in vile deeds all others past and present, both in quality and quantity, the people he exterminated and the lands he laid waste were countless.

The captain who went by sea committed, before he died, some great robberies and outrages, winnowing the people in the coastal towns, people who came out to welcome him with gifts in the kingdom of Yucatán, which is on the route to Naco and Guatemala. After he arrived there he sent out captains in command of many troops throughout all the land, to pillage and kill and raze the towns. There was one captain who made off with three hundred troops and penetrated into the interior for more than one hundred and twenty leagues toward Guatemala, destroying, pillaging, and burning everything in his way. The troops sent to follow him saw the whole land laid waste. But shortly the captain–general who had sent out this rascal died, and there was a succession of other tyrants, all of them merciless, all of them committing frightful cruelties, capturing Indians, selling them as slaves to the ships that were laden with cargoes of wine and clothing and other things. With such actions in the years between one thousand five hundred and twenty-four and one thousand five hundred and thirty-five, they destroyed the provinces of Naco and Honduras, which had been the most populous and fertile lands that could exist in the world.

And now as we cross these lands we see them so deserted and destroyed that anyone, no matter how hardened, would have his heart torn with grief. In those eleven years more than two hundred thousand souls were killed, leaving today on more than a hundred square leagues of land no more than two thousand, and these, each day, are being killed in the aforementioned servitude.

Turning back the clock, I will now speak at greater length of the captain–general who invaded the kingdom of Guatemala which, as I have said, exceeded in size and population all the other kingdoms of the past and present time, extending four hundred leagues south of the Mexican border (which was the route taken), and as this captain–general himself wrote in a letter to the prince who sent him, he massacred and pillaged and burned and devastated all the land wherever he went, considering it his right, as I have said, to subject the native peoples to the inhuman and unjust Spaniards, doing all this in the name of the King of Spain, who was unknown to these peoples and never seen or heard of by them. And without even letting them have time to reflect and deliberate, the Spaniards, almost as soon as their messengers arrived with a warning, began their brutal attacks.

THE PROVINCE AND KINGDOM OF GUATEMALA

When he arrived in said kingdom, he carried out in the first attack a great massacre of the people. And this, in spite of the fact that the chief ruler and other nobles had come out to welcome him, borne in litters, accompanied by trumpets and timbrels, and they celebrated the arriving Spaniards with many fiestas at the gates of the capital city of Ultatlán,[24] where they placed everything at the disposal of the captain–general. They had entertained the Spaniards with especially lavish banquets, and had given them all they asked for and more.

The Spaniards slept that night outside the city, which seemed safer to them, for they thought they might be in danger had they slept inside the city. Next day they summoned the chief ruler and many nobles, and when they came like tame sheep they were seized and commanded to furnish the Christians with a certain weight of gold. The Indians replied that they did not have it to give, because their land lacked gold. The Spaniards then had them burnt alive, without trial or sentencing.

And when the people saw that their chief ruler and the nobles of all those provinces had been slain for no other reason than that they could not provide the gold asked of them, they left their villages and fled to hide in the mountains, and ordered their servants to go to the Spaniards and serve them as their lords, but telling them that they must not reveal where their masters were hidden. And all the common people came to the Spaniards and said they would serve them.

The response made by this pious captain–general was that he could not receive them into his service until they had revealed where their masters were hidden, and that otherwise he would kill them all. The Indians said they did not know where their masters were, but surely their masters' wives and children must know and they were still in their houses, therefore the Spaniards could go there and do with them as they liked. The Indians repeated this many times. And, marvelous to relate, the Spaniards went to the villages where the poor people worked at their tasks, living with their wives and children, confident of their safety. And there the Spaniards attacked them with swords and cut them to pieces.

Another incident of unprovoked cruelty was when the Spaniards entered a large and prosperous town no better guarded than another, and in the course of two hours almost destroyed it, putting to the sword men, women, and children and the aged and infirm who could not manage to escape.

When the Indians saw that humility and the offering of

gifts were of no avail to soften the hearts of the Spaniards, and that patience and endurance were useless, and that without any appearance or color of reason they would be attacked and slain, they agreed to assemble and stand together and die in a war, revenging themselves as best they could against the cruel and infernal enemies; since they well knew that being not only unarmed but naked they would be opposing ferocious men on horseback so well armored that to prevail against them would be impossible, they conceived the idea of digging holes in the middle of the roads, into which the horsemen would fall and have their bellies pierced by the sharp sticks with which the holes would be filled, covered over with turf and weeds. Once or twice horsemen did fall into the holes, but not more than that, for the Spaniards learned how to avoid them. But to avenge themselves against the Indians they threw into those holes all the Indians they could capture of every age and kind. And thus children and old men and even pregnant women and women but lately in childbed were thrown in and perished. As many Indians as could be seized were flung into those holes to be mortally wounded on the sharp sticks; a pitiful sight, especially the women and children. All the remaining Indians were slain with pikes or swords, or were thrown to the savage dogs, which tore them to pieces and devoured them.

Whenever the Spaniards captured an important noble or chieftain, they did him the honor of burning him at the stake. This butchery lasted for close to seven years, from the year twenty-four to the year thirty or thirty-one. You can judge what would be the number of victims that were swallowed up in the holocaust.

An infinite number of vile actions against the Indians were carried out by that miserable tyrant in conjunction with his brothers (for they were no less inhuman and hardhearted than he or the other tyrants who aided him). It was more than enough what those Spaniards did in the province of Cuzocatán where the Villa San Salvador is situated, or is at least in the vicinity. It was a felicitous land bordering the coast of the southern sea, extending a distance of forty or fifty leagues, and in the capital city of Cuzocatán the Indians gave the Spaniards a great welcome, more than twenty or thirty thousand coming out with gifts of live chickens and cooked foods. In response to this welcome, the captain–general ordered each of his officers to take as many Indians as they liked to serve them as cargo bearers. Each Spaniard then took one to five hundred Indians they needed to be well served, and the innocent Indians endured being allocated in this way and they served the Spaniards faultlessly, wholeheartedly, revering them.

Meanwhile the captain–general commanded the Indians to bring him gold, much gold, for that was mainly what he had come there for. The Indians replied that they would gladly provide the Spaniards with all the gold they possessed, and they gathered together a large quantity of copper axes overlaid with a coating of gold, giving them the aspect of solid gold. The captain then had the gold assayed and when it was found that the axes were of copper, he exclaimed: "To the devil with this land! There is no gold here," and he commanded his men to put the Indians that served them in chains and branded as slaves. This was done and to all the Indians they could lay hands on, and I saw one of the sons of the ruler of that city being chained and branded. Some Indians escaped, and when the Indians of the land heard of this great misfortune, they gathered together and took up arms and in the battle that followed, the Spaniards massacred and tortured a great number of Indians. Then they built a city which has now, by divine justice, been destroyed in three deluges, one of water, another of muddy earth, the third of stones larger than thirteen oxen.[25]

When the Spaniards had killed all the chieftains and all the Indians capable of making war, they cast all the others into infernal servitude. And when the Spaniards demanded tribute-slaves, they gave them their sons and daughters, the only slaves they had. These the Spaniards sent by shiploads down the coast to be sold in Peru.

Thus, with massacres and other outrages they laid waste a kingdom extending for more than one hundred square leagues, a land that had been among the most flourishing and populous in the whole world.

And this very same tyrant has written that the land of Guatemala was even more populous than Mexico, which is the truth. But he and his brothers and other Spaniards have slain four or five million souls in fifteen or sixteen years from the year twenty-four to the year forty, and they are still killing and destroying those who survived, and they will go on killing.

Now, it was the habit of this captain–general, when he was about to make war on a town or province to take with him ten or twenty thousand already subjected Indians and set them to fight the Indians in the town or province he intended to invade. And since he did not provide food for his Indians he gave them permission to eat the enemy Indians they captured. And thus he had, in his royal kingdom, a butchery of human beings, where, in his presence, children were killed, cooked, and eaten, and where men were killed merely for their hands and feet which were esteemed as delicacies. And since these inhumanities were occurring in other parts of the Indies, the Indians knew not where to hide. They killed a countless number of Indians in the course of shipbuilding. They also took Indians aboard for voyages to the north and south along the coast. The Indians had to carry anchors to the coast weighing three or four quintals,[26] and they marched, thus shackled, those pathetic naked creatures, one behind the other, their hands clinging to the shoulders and waist of the one in front, carrying heavy burdens on their backs. And I saw many Indians thus laden, struggling in anguish down the roads.

The Spaniards broke up marriages, separating husbands and wives, robbed couples of their children, took for themselves the wives and daughters of the people, or gave them to the sailors and soldiers as consolation, and the sailors bore them away on their vessels that were crowded with Indians, all of them dying of hunger and thirst. And truth to say, if one wanted to tell about this in detail or to describe all the cruelties perpetrated, it would make a big book that would horrify the world.

families broken up

This captain had two fleets built, many ships in each one, and with these he set ablaze, as if with fire from Heaven, the entire coastal land. Oh! How many orphans did he make, how many families did he rob of their sons, how many husbands did he deprive of their wives, how many women did he leave without husbands, how many adulteries and rapes and other acts of violence did he commit! How many did he deprive of liberty, how much anguish, how many calamities did the Indians suffer because of him! How many tears were shed, how many groans were uttered, how many people were left alone, how many were condemned to eternal servitude because of him! And not only Indians in great number but also unfortunate Christians who, in his company, perpetrated grave deeds, how many sins and detestable abominations! And may God have mercy on their souls and be satisfied with the vile ending He gave that tyrant.[27]

Pánuco and Jalisco

With these great cruelties and massacres carried out in the land of Guatemala, it is now proper to speak of the provinces of Pánuco[28] and of the other tyrant, equally insensitive and ruthless, who came to power in the year one thousand five hundred and twenty-five. He continued perpetrating the many cruel acts of his predecessor, putting in irons a great many Indians he enslaved, men who had been as free as I am, and sending them on many ships to the islands of Cuba and Hispaniola where they could be easily sold. And sometimes it happened on those islands that eighty Indians, rational souls, would be traded for a mare.

At this time it was decreed that the city of Mexico and all of New Spain should be governed by other tyrants and lawmakers with this tyrant presiding above them. And he, with the others, committed many lawless acts, sins, and cruelties, thefts, and abominations hard to believe. With which actions they finally depopulated the land, and if God had not put a stop to it by the resistance of the Franciscan friars and then with the new provisions of a Royal Audiencia,[29] good provisions, friendly to every virtue, within a few years they would have left New Spain as devastated as the island of Hispaniola.

One man, among that company of Spaniards, wanting to wall in an orchard he had acquired, brought in about one thousand Indians and set them to work without pay and without giving them anything to eat. The Indians died, dropping dead of hunger, one by one, and he paid no attention to this.

Then the tyrant-Governor, overlord of these tyrants, had a new idea. After he had devastated Pánuco and after the said good Royal Audiencia had taken place, he had the notion of penetrating farther into the interior to find new land to tyrannize, and he took with him from the city of Mexico a force of fifteen or twenty thousand Indians to carry the burdens of himself and his Spanish comrades. Of all those many Indians only two hundred survived, all the others having with reason died on that long march to the southern province of Mechuacam,[30] some forty leagues distant from the city of Mexico, another felicitous country, filled with people, like Mexico. The King came out to welcome him, with a large company in a procession, offering gifts and offering their services.

The Spaniards immediately took him captive and put

him to the torture, for he was reputed to have a large store of gold and silver and other treasures. They stretched his body between two branches of a tree and placed a burning brazier under his feet and a boy, with a swab dipped in oil, sprinkled the soles of his feet from time to time to roast them well, while a cruel soldier kept his arbalest aimed at the victim's heart and another excited a savage dog to attack the tortured man. And in a trice the dog amputated his hands. To this, a Franciscan friar bore witness. And from all these torments the Indian King soon perished.

In this kind of torture and killing a great many chieftains and caciques were put to death in that province, the Spaniards acting thus to extort from them their treasures of silver and gold. One Spanish tyrant[31] while making his way to rob the houses and the ranches of the Indians, more with a view to robbing than to killing or capturing, heard that some of the people kept their golden idols concealed and he and his company of Spaniards, who had not mentioned the true Faith or the one God to these people, held and tortured the chieftains until the idols were disclosed. And when the Spaniards saw that they had mistakenly been informed that the idols were of gold, they felt defrauded and forced the caciques to buy back the idols with what gold and silver treasure they had. The chieftains did this after being tortured cruelly, and took back their idols to worship them. These are examples of the acts of the Spaniards in the Indies which dishonor the name of God.

The same great captain–general then left Mechuacam to go to Jalisco,[32] which was as populous as a beehive and a felicitous land, admired for its fertility, a settlement extending for almost seven leagues. As the Spaniards entered, the chieftains and the people came out to welcome them with gifts and celebrations, as was the custom throughout the Indies.

And the cruelties and wickedness began again as usual, since all the Spaniards there had become used to them, always with the aim God had allowed them, which was to obtain gold. They burnt the towns, captured the caciques, inflicted torture, enslaved many. They took away with them many captives in chains, loaded down with heavy burdens, launching them out on the roads where many of them perished, for the burdens were too heavy for them, weak as they were from hunger.

One Spaniard took a maiden by force to commit the sin of the flesh with her, dragging her away from her mother, finally having to unsheath his sword to cut off the woman's hands and when the damsel still resisted they stabbed her to death.

Among many other things, this tyrant put the slaves in irons, unjustly, for the Indians were free people, all of them, some four thousand five hundred of the captives, men, women, and children, taking infants from their mothers' breasts, capturing children one and two and three years old. Yet these people had come out to welcome the Spaniards in peace. In this province the Spaniards committed too many vile deeds to count.

Finally, with countless iniquitous wars and massacres the entire land was placed in the usual pestilential servitude to which the Christians in the Indies are wont to subject these peoples. Yet in these conditions they set themselves up as the stewards of the people. And these stewards commit all their unheard-of cruelties to extract gold and tributes from the Indians. These stewards slew many Indians by hanging, burning, and being torn to pieces by savage dogs, also by cutting off the hands and feet and heads and tongues, and for no other reason than to spread terror and induce the Indians to give them gold and tributes. And that egregious tyrant well knew that these things would have been given without all those floggings, beatings, buffetings and all the cruelties that were practiced every day and every hour.

It is said of this tyrant that he destroyed eight hundred towns, burning them to the ground in the kingdom of Jalisco, and this caused some desperadoes among the Indians to flee to the mountains, having seen so many of their people be cruelly put to death. From their hiding place in the mountains these Indians justly and rightly attacked and killed a few Spaniards.

And after this many other offenses and outrages were committed by other tyrants who passed through the land on their way to discover, as they said, new lands. These assembled many Indians to build forts in cliffy regions, and those forts still stand. And now once more they are perpetrating such great cruelties that they have almost ended up by depopulating and laying waste all that great land, killing a countless number of people. And those wretches, those Spaniards, blinded by greed, think they have the God-given right to perpetrate all these cruelties and cannot see that the Indians have cause, have abundant causes, to attack them and by force of arms, if they had weapons, to throw them out of their lands, this under all the laws, natural, human, and divine. And they cannot see the injustice of their acts, the iniquity of the injuries and inexpiable sins they have committed against the Indians, and they renew their wars, thinking and saying that the victories they have had against the Indians, laying waste the lands, have all been approved by God and they praise Him, like the thieves of whom the prophet Zechariah speaks: "Feed the flock of the slaughter; whose possessors slay them, and hold themselves not guilty: and they that sell them say, Blessed be the Lord; for I am rich."[33]

THE KINGDOM OF YUCATAN

In the year one thousand five hundred and twenty-six, another wretch of a Spanish tyrant was provided to govern the kingdom of Yucatán,[34] thanks to the lies and falsehoods he told and the presents he gave to the King of Spain, as has been the case of all the other tyrants sent to govern the Indies down to this day; thus they are given charges and rank that will enable them to rob the native peoples.

The kingdom of Yucatán was filled with countless inhabitants because it has a healthy climate where food is abundant and where fruits and honey abound; there is more honey and beeswax in Yucatán than in any other part of the Indies until now visited. This kingdom is three hundred leagues in circumference. The people of Yucatán were noted for their prudence, their good order, their lack of vices; they were very worthy to be brought to the knowledge of God. It was a kingdom where great Spanish cities could have been built, where people could have lived in an earthly Paradise, had the Spaniards been worthy. But the cities were not built, because of the greed, the sinfulness, the insensitivity of the Spaniards. They were not worthy, as they were not worthy of the many other parts of the Indies, as has been shown.

This new tyrant-Governor had with him three hundred men and they waged ruthless war against these good and innocent people who lived quietly in their houses, in no way offending anyone. The Spaniards massacred countless numbers.

But there was no gold in this kingdom, or if there had been at one time it had all been taken out of the mines. However, gold could be made of those bodies and souls for whom Jesus Christ died, and the Spaniards assembled all the Indians they had allowed to survive and sent them away on the many ships that came, attracted by the smell of slaves. They would be traded for wine and vinegar and pigs and clothing and for horses or anything else needed by the tyrant and his followers, or what they deemed necessary.

And the Spaniards were allowed to choose, among one hundred and fifty Indian maidens the ones they liked best, paying for each one an arroba of wine or oil or vinegar or pigs, and the same for a comely boy chosen from among one or two hundred. And it sometimes happened that a boy who appeared to be the son of a noble would be traded for a whole cheese and a hundred of them for a horse.

In such actions the Spaniards were engaged from the year twenty-six to the year thirty-three, which was seven years spent in despoiling and exterminating the inhabitants of this land, and they went on killing until news came of the wealth in Peru, to which the Spaniards then went, ending for a short time the infernal conditions in Yucatán.

But then the tyrant's ministers returned to perpetrate still more outrages against the Indians and offenses against God, and these things they are still doing today now that they have depopulated the entire three hundred leagues of this kingdom which were, as we have said, teeming with inhabitants.

It would be hard to make anyone believe, and harder still to narrate, the infamous deeds in all their details. One incident may suffice. As the Spanish wretches went about with their savage dogs trying to terrorize the Indians, men and women alike, one woman (thinking to soften the hearts of the Spaniards) tied her year-old child to her foot and hanged herself from a beam. No sooner had she done this than the dogs arrived and tore the child to pieces. It must be added that a Franciscan friar baptized the child before it died.

As the Spaniards prepared to depart from this kingdom, one of them told the son of a chieftain of a certain village to come with them. The boy said No, he did not want to leave his country. The Spaniard responded: "Come with us, otherwise I will cut off your ears." The boy still said No, he did not want to leave his land. The Spaniard unsheathed his dagger and cut off the boy's ears, first one, then the other. And when the boy said again that he did not want to leave his land, the Spaniard cut off his nose, laughing as he did so, as if he had administered a punishment as trifling as to pull the boy's hair.

This Godforsaken man boasted about this act in front of a venerable religious, and also said that he worked as hard as he could to get Indian women with child, for when he sold them as slaves he would be paid more if they were pregnant.

One day, and this incident happened either in the kingdom of Yucatán or in New Spain, a certain Spaniard went hunting for stags or rabbits and, finding no game, and wanting to satisfy his dogs, he took a baby from its Indian mother and with his sword sliced off the child's arms and legs for the dogs to share, then after that meal on those pieces of flesh, he[35] threw down the little body for all the dogs to share. Observe in this incident the insensitivity of the Spaniards who call themselves Christians in this land, and see how they have brought the one true God into opprobrium, *in reprobus sensus,* and in what esteem they hold these peoples created in the image of God and redeemed by the blood of the Savior. And we shall see even worse things later on.

Leaving aside the countless unheard-of cruelties perpetrated in this kingdom by those men who call themselves Christians, acts which no sane mind can judge to be justified, I will conclude with only these words: When these damnable tyrants left this kingdom to go to Peru, they were moved by the greed that blinded them, being avid for the riches of Peru. The Franciscan friar, Father Jacobo, bestirred himself to accompany the Spaniards, taking with him four religious of the Order of San Francisco, to preach and to bring the tidings of Jesus Christ to the remnants of those Indians, survivors of the infernal harvest the Spaniards had carried out in the span of seven years.

I believe it was in the year one thousand five hundred and thirty-four, that those friars were sent into the presence of certain Indians of the province of Mexico as messengers to find out if the Indians thought it well for them to enter the land to bring tidings of the one true God and our Lord and Savior, only God of the world. They called a council of all the village chiefs, after gathering what information they could about the kind of men these were who called themselves friars and what it was they pretended to be and in what way they differed from the Christians who had inflicted so much suffering on them. Finally they welcomed them and said they could stay, provided they would not be accompanied by any other Spaniards. The friars promised to abide by this ruling, which had been approved by the Viceroy of New Spain, who had also pledged that no other Spaniards would enter the kingdom except those of religious Orders, and had guaranteed that no injuries would be perpetrated by the religious.

And so they preached the Gospel of Christ as it should be preached and the Indians learned the articles of the Faith and about the Kings of Spain who were their sovereign rulers. And the religious gave so much love and relish to their work and set such good examples that the Indians were glad to learn about these things for never in the seven years since the Spaniards had come there had they been told that there was another King besides the one there, who ravished and betrayed the land and its people. And at the end of forty days of preaching, the Indians took the friars to show them their idols, handing them over to be burned, and afterward took the friars to meet their sons and tell them about the burning of the idols for they wanted their sons, who were the apple of their eyes, to hear the friars preach.

And they built churches and temples and houses, and other provinces invited the Franciscan friars to bring them the tidings of the one true God and to tell them about the great Kings of Castile and how they should accept the Emperor as their supreme and universal sovereign. And the chieftains made certain marks on the parchment (where all this was set down in writing) as their signatures, said parchment being in my possession along with the testimonies of the Franciscan friars.

Then something occurred that was and still is unique in the annals of the Indies, no matter what falsehoods the tyrants tell. Persuaded by the Franciscan friars, twelve or fifteen noble chieftains, each having much land and many vassals, each one acting on his own account, assembled their vassals and taking their votes, he and they declared themselves subjects of the King of Castile and recognized the Emperor as their supreme and universal ruler.

Then, while the Franciscan friars were rejoicing at this progress in the Christian Faith and were full of hope that they would bring all the inhabitants of the land to Jesus Christ—all the inhabitants who had survived the unjust wars and massacres, which were not a few—there entered the land at another point eighteen Spanish horsemen and twelve foot soldiers, a total of thirty, bringing many loads of idols taken from Indians in other provinces. And the captain of the thirty Spaniards summoned an Indian noble in that part of the kingdom, and told him to take the loads of idols and distribute them throughout the land, trading each idol for an Indian man or woman to give to the Spaniards and be sold into slavery. They threatened the chief, saying that if he refused to do this, they would make war on him. And he, impelled by fear, distributed the idols on his own land and commanded all his vassals to take and worship them and to give a son and a daughter to be sold into slavery. The Indians obeyed in fear, and he who had two sons gave one of them, and he who had three sons gave two, and in this manner the great sacrifice was accomplished and the noble chief or cacique was able to satisfy the Spanish Christians.

One of those impious and thievish Spaniards, on the point of death shortly afterward, by name Juan García, summoned his maidservant and told her there was a load of idols under his bed and that she should not trade them for poultry because those idols were valuable, and that she must trade them for slaves. Then, with this last will and testament, the rascal died. Can anyone doubt that he was not borne away by the devil and is burning in hell?

Pause now to consider what progress in religion can be made with such examples of Christians as the Spaniards who go out to the Indies. What honor do they procure for the true God? What effort do they make to bring the knowledge of God to the Indians and bring them to worship Him? What care do they take of those souls to plant the seed of faith and have it grow and burgeon? And judge whether what they did was less sinful than that of Jeroboam who "drove Israel from following the Lord and made them sin a great sin."[36] Or is it equal to or more than the sin committed by Judas, and did it not create a greater disturbance?

Such, then, are the works of the Spaniards who go out to the Indies for greed of gold and who, in truth, have sold people into slavery countless times, and who are still doing so, and who deny and resist Jesus Christ.

When the Indians saw there was no true escape, that although the Franciscan friars had promised them no other Spaniards would enter their provinces, there had entered a number of Spaniards bringing into their country idols from other lands to sell, while they themselves had burned their idols, for they had been ready to worship the true God. And they rose up in angry revolt and the entire population joined them in opposition to the Franciscan friars. Some Indians came to them saying, "Why did you lie to us, falsely telling us that no other Christians would enter our lands? And now they have come to sell us the gods of other provinces and other nations. And why did you burn our gods? Were not our gods better than theirs?"

The Franciscans pacified them as best they could and they sought out the thirty Spaniards, telling them of the damage they had done and asking them to leave the country. This the Spaniards refused to do, and they told the Indians that the friars had asked them to come, which was a consummate lie. Finally the Indians decided to kill the friars and the friars, having been warned, managed to flee one night.

But after they had gone, the Indians, remembering the innocence of the Franciscan friars, so different from the wickedness of the Spanish soldiers, sent some messengers to find them, imploring forgiveness for having caused them to leave and asking them to return. And the friars, zealous for the salvation of those souls, believed them and returned, and were welcomed like angels, the Indians rendering them a thousand services. And they remained there for four or five months. But since the Christian Spaniards who had entered the land would not leave it, nor could the Viceroy make them leave, no matter how hard he tried, because this land was at a distance from New Spain (although the Viceroy had them proscribed as traitors), and because those Spaniards unceasingly continued to injure and oppress the Indians, it appeared to the friars that sooner or later, as a result of those wicked acts, the Indians would turn against them once more, especially since it was no longer possible to preach the word of God without incidents caused by the wicked Spaniards. And so they decided to vacate the land, which would thus remain without the light and succor of the doctrine and those souls would remain irremediably in darkness and ignorance and misery, deprived of the knowledge of God that they had been avidly acquiring. It was like depriving newly rooted plants of water. And all this because of the inexpiable culpability of those wicked Spaniards.

THE PROVINCE OF SANTA MARTA

The province of Santa Marta[37] and bordering lands were rich in gold, and here the Indians had the energy and ability to extract it from the mines. For this reason, the Spanish tyrants, since the year one thousand four hundred and ninety-eight, have done nothing but attack and rob and kill the inhabitants, sending ships to attack the coast again and again, causing great havoc. And with the massacres and remarkable cruelties this continual ravaging of the coast had devastated more than four hundred leagues of land by the year one thousand five hundred and twenty-three.

In that year, Spanish tyrants were established here,[38] and because, as we have said, this region was rich in gold, there was a succession of captains–general, each one outdoing the other in cruelties, as if they had vowed to commit ever greater outrages, for truly their excesses proved the rule we have expounded.

In the year one thousand five hundred and twenty-nine there arrived a very great tyrant with a large company of men devoid of fear of God or any compassion. He perpetrated many impieties, and the massacres he carried out went far beyond anything that had occurred before. In the course of the six or seven years he was in this land, he pillaged and robbed the people of many great treasures. He died without confession, obliged to flee from the official residence. He was succeeded by other tyrants, all of them evil-doers, who robbed the few people who had survived the bloody knives and hands of the past tyrants.

These tyrants extended their power into the interior, laying waste large provinces, massacring and taking captive a great number of people, administering frightful tortures on nobles and vassals alike, all in the effort to discover the villages that had gold, and their excesses in cruelty, both as to number and kind, surpassed, as we have said, anything that had gone before. From the year one thousand five hundred and twenty-nine to the present day, there has been devastated in this region an extent of land measuring more than four hundred leagues, which, like the other provinces of the Indies, had held numerous inhabitants.

In truth I can affirm that were I to recount the vile acts committed here, the exterminations, the massacres, the cruelties, the violence and sinfulness against God and the King of Spain, I would write a very big book. But this will have to wait for another time, God willing. Here I want only to repeat a few of the words written today to our lord the King by the Bishop of this province, in a letter dated the twentieth of May in the year one thousand five hundred and forty-one, which says, among other things:

I wish to say, great Caesar, that the means to remedy this land is for Your Majesty to remove from power these rascally stepfathers and to give the land a husband who will treat her with the reasonableness she deserves. And this must be done rapidly, for otherwise, the way she is being harassed and fatigued by these tyrants that have charge of her, I hold it a certainty that very soon she will die.

And further on the letter reads:

Then Your Majesty will clearly see how those who govern her deserve to lose their governorship, in order to alleviate the conditions in these republics. And if this is not done, my view is that there is no cure for the infirmities of these lands.

Your Majesty will find out that there are no Christians in these lands; instead, there are demons. There are neither servants of God or of the King. Because, in truth, the great obstacle to my being able to bring the Indians from war-making to a peaceful way of life, and to bringing the knowledge of God to those Indians who are peaceful is the harsh and cruel treatment of these Indians by the Spanish Christians. For which scabrous and bitter reason no word can be more hateful to those Indians than the word Christian, which they render in their language as Yares, meaning Demons. And without a doubt they are right, because the actions of these Governors are neither Christian nor humane but are actions of the devil.

Hence, the Indians, seeing those vile actions of men so lacking in piety, they form the idea that the Christians obey the laws of the devil who is their God and King. And struggling as I do to persuade them of anything else is like trying to dry up the ocean. It gives them cause to laugh and to mock Jesus Christ and His law. And as the war-making Indians see the treatment meted out to the peace-loving Indians, they think it better to die in battle than to die many times under the dominion of the Spaniards. I know this, invincible Caesar, from experience.

Still further down in this letter we find:

Your Majesty has more servants in the Indies than is known to Your Majesty, because there is not one soldier among the many here who does not publicly boast that when he breaks in or robs or destroys or kills or burns the vassals of Your Majesty, it is because he wants to be given gold for Your Majesty. And thus it would be well, O most Christian Caesar, that Your Majesty let it be known, while punishing some of them severely, that such services which are a disservice to God, will not be accepted.

The above statements are formulated in the words of the aforementioned Bishop of Santa Marta, through which can be clearly seen what is now being done in all these unfortunate lands against innocent people. He calls hostile or war-making the Indians who are able to escape and take refuge in the mountains. And he calls peaceful the Indians who, after the death of countless unfortunates of their nation, place themselves at the disposal of the tyrants and the horrible servitude we have mentioned. The Spaniards finally kill off those peaceful Indians, who die of hunger, as appears in the statements of the Bishop. But in truth he explains very little about the sufferings they endure.

It should be told that the Indians of this land, when they weary and sink down, fainting under the heavy loads they are made to carry, are buffeted and kicked by the Spaniards, who break their teeth with blows from their sword hilts. Then the Indians get up, out of breath, and continue their march, saying, "Oh, wicked people, I can do no more! Kill me, I want to leave my dead body here." They say this with loud groans and clutching their breasts, in pain and anguish.

Oh, who can bear to hear about even one such affliction these harmless people are enduring at the hands of the dastardly Spaniards! And such things are told in a hundred parts of the country. May God give understanding to those who can and will remedy this situation.

THE PROVINCE OF CARTAGENA

This province of Cartagena extends fifty leagues to the south of Santa Marta and to the west, contiguous with the province of Canú to the Gulf of Urabá, hugging the coast for a hundred leagues. And it includes much land in the interior, to the south. The people of this province have been afflicted and killed. The land has been laid waste over the years from one thousand four hundred and ninety-eight until today, as was Santa Marta. The Spaniards have perpetrated some outstanding cruelties on these islands. There have been many massacres. Here I will not dwell on the killings, the pillage, the many acts of wickedness, but will merely say that on Cartagena were perpetrated the same acts as in other parts.

THE COAST OF PEARLS, PARIA AND THE ISLAND OF TRINIDAD

Along the coast of Paria as far as the Gulf of Venezuela, a distance of two hundred leagues,[39] the destruction carried out by the Spaniards has been noteworthy. They have attacked and have taken alive as many people as they could, to sell them as slaves. The Spaniards often take captives into their houses, as domestic servants, treating them well for a time, treating them like sons and daughters, the captives regarding the Spaniards like fathers, and serving them to the best of their ability. Then the Spaniards after a while betray their trust. It is painful to tell of how many injuries are then inflicted on these people by the Spaniards, ever since they invaded the coastal region in the year one thousand five hundred and ten and down to the present time. I will recount only two or three instances of cruelty, from which can be judged the other innumerable and hideous acts deserving all the fires of hell.

On the island of Trinidad, which is much larger than

Sicily and much more felicitous, close to the mainland at Paria, is where the Indians are the best to be found in the Indies, as to goodness and virtues. The Spanish tyrant, with sixty or seventy men, all rascals and experienced thieves, sent a messenger to proclaim that they had come to dwell on the island in peace with the Indians. The people welcomed them as if they were kinsmen, as if they were their sons, and treated them with cheerful kindness, serving them, bringing them gifts and giving them their surplus food, as is the custom in the Indies, everywhere. They gave generously of all the products needed by the Spaniards, and they built a big house, large enough to accommodate all of them, according to the desire expressed by the Spaniards who said they wanted to live together, but in reality it was because of a plan they had, which they soon carried out. When the double roof of straw was made, so that those within could not see outside, they had as many Indians as possible come into the house, with the pretense that they were needed to do some finishing work, then the Spaniards posted guards so that no one could leave, the guards standing with unsheathed swords. Then they forbade the Indians to make a move, and tied them up, and whenever one of the Indians tried to escape he was cut to pieces.

Some of the Indians managed to escape, either wounded or unharmed, and they, with the villagers who had not entered the house, seized another house and with bows and arrows defended themselves against the Spaniards until the Christians set fire to the house, burning to death all the Indians inside it.

Then, with their captives who numbered one hundred

and eighty or two hundred, the Spaniards went down to their ships, hoisted sail and voyaged to San Juan, where half the number of Indians were sold as slaves, after which they voyaged to Hispaniola where the remainder of the captives were sold.

When I remonstrated with the captain–general for such outstanding acts of wickedness and betrayal, as I encountered him in San Juan, his response was this: "Sir, after all, I have only obeyed the orders I was given when I was sent to the Indies, for I was told 'If you cannot conquer them by war, then capture them, no matter how.' " And he told me that, in truth, he had all his life lacked a mother and father and had never been treated kindly except by the Indians on the island of Trinidad. He said this to explain his great confusion and the worsening of his sins which had been many on the mainland, and now the taking captive Indians to whom he had promised safety.

See what acts were these: capturing Indians to sell them into slavery.

On another occasion, our Dominican Order having been given permission to preach and convert the native peoples who were without enlightenment and hope of salvation, they sent a religious eminently learned in theology and of great virtue and holiness, along with a lay friar to survey the land and to find with the help of an Indian a site favorable to the establishment of a monastery. They were welcomed like angels from Heaven upon their arrival in a settlement and their words were listened to with attention, devotion, and good cheer. By words I mean their gestures, for they mainly used sign language, not knowing or understanding the language of the Indians.

By chance, after the ship that brought them had gone away, another vessel came and the Spaniards on it, using their customary deceitfulness, took on board the chief ruler of these lands, without the knowledge of the Dominican friars. The ruler's name was Don Alonso, which was either a name the Dominican friars had given him or had been given by some other Spaniards, since the Indians are very fond of being called by a Christian name, asking for and being given one even before they know enough of the Faith to be baptized. Thus, the Spaniards duped the aforesaid Don Alonso into boarding the ship with his wife and a certain number of his followers, and there they celebrated a fiesta. Finally the Spaniards persuaded seventeen other Indians to board the ship, which they did, confident that because the Dominican religious were in their land the Spaniards would not harm them. Once they had the Indians on board, the traitorous Spaniards hoisted sail and voyaged to Hispaniola where all the captives were sold into slavery.

All the people of the land, upon seeing their chief ruler and his wife borne away, came to the Dominican friars, intending to kill them. The friars, confronted with such an act of wickedness, were so full of anguish that they wanted to die, being ready to give their lives in reparation for such an act of wickedness, especially since this unjust act was a hindrance to their preaching the word of God to the Indians. They soothed the Indians as best they could, assuring them that by the next ship they would send a letter to Hispaniola and would have the Indian chief and

his followers returned to this land. Then God brought a
ship to that place, in confirmation of the damnation of
those that governed, and the Dominican friars wrote
many times asking for the return of the Indians who had
been so unjustly taken captive. But those who read the
letters were never willing to do justice, because to some
among them had been allocated their share of those Indians who had so wickedly been taken captive by the tyrants.

The two friars had promised the Indians that within
four months they would see their chieftain, Don Alonso,
return with his wife and followers, so when they did not
return either within four months or eight months, the
Indians became restless and the friars prepared to give
their lives, as they had offered to do before. And the
Indians thus took a just vengeance on these innocents
when they slew them. Because the Indians thought the
Dominicans had been the cause of the betrayal, and because they had seen no truth in their promise that within
four months their chief would return, and because until
then (as today) the Indians could see no difference between the friars and the Spanish tyrants, thieves, and bul-
lies wreaking havoc everywhere in this land. Without a
doubt the blessed friars suffered unjustly and thus, according to our holy Faith, they are, as true martyrs, with God
in Heaven, blessed martyrs who willingly came to the
Indies, in obedience to their Order, to preach and expound
the holy Faith and save all those souls and to endure
whatever labors or sufferings were offered them for the
sake of our crucified Lord, Jesus Christ.

Once again, on account of the wicked Christians and

their nefarious acts, Indians had killed another two friars, this time of the Order of St. Dominic's Friars Preachers and one Franciscan, in which death I was a witness and by a divine miracle escaped death myself, the story of which would fill men with terror. But the story is too long to describe here, it must wait for the Day of Judgment when everything will be made clear and God will revenge such outrageous offenses as are committed by the Spaniards in the Indies, by Spaniards who call themselves Christians.

And again, in these provinces on that part of the Venezuelan coast called Cape Codera, there was a village ruled by a chief called Higoroto,[40] a proper name common among these peoples. He was so good and his people so virtuous that when a great number of Spaniards came in ships they were given help in repairs, food, rest, care, and comfort. These Indians felt safe from the kind of death they heard about from those who fled into their province where many tyrannies had caused much affliction. Higoroto sent these survivors to the nearby Island of Pearls,[41] where were many Christians, instead of killing them as he could have done. And all the Christians in the village ruled by Higoroto called it "the house and home" of everyone. And a wretch of a Spanish tyrant decided to attack this village.

They sent a ship and invited many Indians to embark on it and, trustingly, many men, women, and children went aboard. Then the Spaniards hoisted sail and voyaged to the island of San Juan, where all the captives were sold as slaves.

I arrived in San Juan at about that same time, and saw

the tyrant and heard of his vile acts. He had left an entire village destroyed, and of all the tyrants that ravaged that coastal country, he was the most abominated, for he destroyed this village which had been a refuge where everyone felt as safe as if in their own house. I repeat: I am omitting a number of wicked deeds and horrifying examples of such destructions perpetrated and still being perpetrated in this land.

They have brought to the island of Hispaniola and the island of San Juan more than two million souls taken captive, and have sent them to do hard larbor in the mines, labors that caused many of them to die. And it is a great sorrow and heartbreak to see this coastal land which was so flourishing, now a depopulated desert.

This is truth that can be verified, for no more do they bring ships loaded with Indians that have been thus attacked and captured as I have related. No more do they cast overboard into the sea the third part of the numerous Indians they stow on their vessels, these dead being added to those they have killed in their native lands, the captives crowded into the holds of their ships, without food or water, or with very little, so as not to deprive the Spanish tyrants who call themselves ship owners and who carry enough food for themselves on their voyages of attack. And for the pitiful Indians who died of hunger and thirst, there is no remedy but to cast them into the sea. And verily, as a Spaniard told me, their ships in these regions could voyage without compass or chart, merely by following for the distance between the Lucayos Islands and Hispaniola, which is sixty or seventy leagues, the trace of those Indian corpses floating in the sea, corpses that had been cast overboard by earlier ships.

Afterward, when they disembark on the island of Hispaniola, it is heartbreaking to see those naked Indians, heartbreaking for anyone with a vestige of piety, the famished state they are in, fainting and falling down, weak from hunger, men, women, old people, and children.

Then, like sheep, they are sorted out into flocks of ten or twenty persons, separating fathers from sons, wives from husbands, and the Spaniards draw lots, the ship owners carrying off their share, the best flock, to compensate them for the moneys they have invested in their fleet of two or three ships, the ruffian tyrants getting their share of captives who will be house slaves, and when in this *"repartimiento"* a tyrant gets an old person or an invalid, he says, "Why do you give me this one? To bury him? And this sick one, do you give him to me to make him well?" See by such remarks in what esteem the Spaniards hold the Indians and judge if they are accomplishing the divine concepts of love for our fellow man, as laid down by the prophets.

The tyranny exercised by the Spaniards against the Indians in the work of pearl fishing is one of the most cruel that can be imagined. There is no life as infernal and desperate in this century that can be compared with it, although the mining of gold is a dangerous and burdensome way of life. The pearl fishers dive into the sea at a depth of five fathoms, and do this from sunrise to sunset, and remain for many minutes without breathing, tearing the oysters out of their rocky beds where the pearls are formed. They come to the surface with a netted bag of these oysters where a Spanish torturer is waiting in a canoe or skiff, and if the pearl diver shows signs of wanting to rest, he is showered with blows, his hair is pulled, and he is thrown back into the water, obliged to continue the hard work of tearing out the oysters and bringing them again to the surface.

The food given the pearl divers is codfish, not very nourishing, and the bread made of maize, the bread of the Indies. At night the pearl divers are chained so they cannot escape.

Often a pearl diver does not return to the surface, for these waters are infested with man-eating sharks of two kinds, both vicious marine animals that can kill, eat, and swallow a whole man.

In this harvesting of pearls let us again consider whether the Spaniards preserve the divine concepts of love for their fellow men, when they place the bodies of the Indians in such mortal danger, and their souls, too, for these pearl divers perish without the holy sacraments. And it is solely because of the Spaniards' greed for gold that they force the Indians to lead such a life, often a brief life, for it is impossible to continue for long diving into the cold water and holding the breath for minutes at a time, repeating this hour after hour, day after day; the continual cold penetrates them, constricts the chest, and they die spitting blood, or weakened by diarrhea.

The hair of these pearl divers, naturally black, is as if burnished by the saltpeter in the water, and hangs down their backs making them look like sea dogs or monsters of another species. And in this extraordinary labor, or, better put, in this infernal labor, the Lucayan Indians are finally consumed, as are captive Indians from other provinces. And all of them were publicly sold for one hundred and fifty castellanos, these Indians who had lived happily on their islands until the Spaniards came, although such a thing was against the law. But the unjust judges did nothing to stop it. For all the Indians of these islands are known to be great swimmers.

THE RIVER YUYAPARI

In the province of Paria rises a river called Yuyapari,[42] which drains more than a hundred leagues of the upper land. One wretch of a Spanish tyrant voyaged for many leagues up this river in the year one thousand five hundred and twenty-nine, with four hundred or more men, and perpetrated great massacres, burning alive and running through with swords countless innocent victims who had been working in their fields or living in their houses without doing anyone harm, not thinking of danger. That tyrant left the province darkened and burnt, abandoned by those who managed to flee. The tyrant finally died, and his fleet was broken up. But other tyrants followed him, perpetrating the same evils and today they go to and fro in this region, destroying, killing, and condemning to eternal damnation the souls the Son of God had shed his blood to redeem.

THE KINGDOM OF VENEZUELA

In the year one thousand five hundred and twenty-six, with the usual dangerous persuasions and deceits to conceal the injuries and losses God and the Indians suffered along with the King in the Indies, the Emperor granted and conceded the government and jurisdiction of the large kingdom of Venezuela, much larger than Spain, to some German merchant adventurers in exchange for certain concessions and agreements. Those merchants,[43] upon entering the land with three hundred or more men, encountered people as tame as sheep, as were all the native peoples in the Indies everywhere, until they suffered injury at the hands of the Spaniards. And here were committed, I believe, incomparably more cruelties than those we have described, acts more irrational and ferocious than any inflicted by the most ferocious lions and tigers and rabid wolves. Because the actions were carried out with more avidity and blind greed, with more subtle determination to rob the Indians of their gold and silver than all the tyrants who had gone before. They subordinated all shame, all fear of God and of the King, forgetting that they were mortal men, having greater freedom, since they possessed all the jurisdiction of the land.

They ravaged, destroyed, incarnadined, and depopulated these dominions extending over more than four hundred leagues that had been supremely happy and admirable provinces, densely populated, rich in gold. Here the conquerors have slain the total population of diverse nations; on many leagues they have not left a single human being alive, except for the few who took refuge in caves, in the bowels of the earth, to escape the alien and pestilential knives. Those German merchants have killed and uprooted innocent generations, employing a variety of strange iniquities and impieties (as I consider them), and they are still, today, unremittingly doing the same thing.

Of the infinite number of offenses and outrages perpetrated in this region, I will give only four or five examples. From these it will be possible to judge the methods that have been used here to effect the devastation and depopulation we have mentioned above.

They captured the supreme ruler of this province, without any cause other than to extract from him gold, through torture. He broke loose and fled to the mountains where he stirred up the people who were hiding there in the underbrush. They hunted down those in revolt and there ensued great slaughters, and all those taken captive were sold openly as slaves. In all the provinces where these conquerors came, no matter where, they were welcomed with songs and dances and gifts of gold in great quantity. And this continued until the conquerors seized the noble ruler of the province. The hospitality of the people was repaid by terror, which spread through the land as the people were put to the sword.

On one occasion, when the Indians came out to welcome the conquerors, they were all placed in a big house of straw and at a command were slaughtered. Some Indians escaped from the bloody hands of those bestial men by climbing the wooden stanchions. The commander then set fire to the house, burning to death all the ones who had escaped death by the sword.

A great many villages were depopulated, the few survivors of the massacres fleeing to the mountains for safety.

The conquerors arrived in a large province bordering the province and kingdom of Santa Marta, where the

Indians were dwelling in peace, occupied at their crafts in their houses, their haciendas, doing their usual work. The conquerors remained for some time in the villages, consuming the Indians' food and provisions, while the Indians served them wholeheartedly, enduring continual oppression and importunities, the intolerably gross behavior of the conquerors, their enormous appetites—one man eating at a single meal more than would suffice for a family of ten Indians in a month.

Of their own free will, the Indians gave them at this time large quantities of gold, and performed countless services of a friendly nature. Finally, wanting to depart, the tyrants decided to repay the Indians in the following way.

The German tyrant who was the Governor (and we believe he was a heretic, for he neither attended Mass nor allowed any of his men or the Indians serving them to attend Mass, the Germans all being Lutherans or known as such), commanded that all the Indians and their wives and children be herded into a huge corral surrounded with stakes which the Indians themselves had driven into the ground. And he commanded that no food be given them until each one had ransomed himself by promising to bring back gold from his house, so much for himself, so much for his wife, so much for his child or children. Many Indians were allowed to go to their houses from which they brought back the required gold. But then the tyrant hired some rascally Spaniards to go to the houses where the ransomed Indians had resumed their lives, and to bring them back to the corral, where they were submitted once more to torture from hunger and thirst, and told they could ransom themselves again for more gold. Some Indians ransomed themselves several times. Others, who had no more gold to give, having given all they possessed, were kept in the corral until they died of hunger.

Thus the German tyrant ravaged and destroyed and depopulated a province rich in gold that had been densely inhabited. And in a large valley of this province, forty leagues in extent, he burnt a settlement comprised of one thousand houses.

This diabolical tyrant decided to push into the interior of Peru, desiring to explore the country for gold. For this unhappy journey he took with him a great number of the surviving Indians chained together, each of them carrying a cargo weighing four arrobas. And when one of the Indians would weaken or faint from hunger and weariness, they cut off his head at the collar of the chain, so as not to delay or stop the march of the others, and the head would fall to one side of the road while the body fell to the other side. And the burden the dead man had carried was distributed among the other captive Indians.

To recount the provinces razed by this tyrant, the towns and settlements he burned, the people he killed, the particular cruelties he perpetrated, and the massacres he carried out on this march into the interior is not possible, and the plain truth is unbelievable.

Other tyrants who succeeded him in Venezuela also followed the route he took into the interior, as did the tyrants in command at Santa Marta, all with the same damnable avid desire to discover a hoard of gold in Peru.[44]

And they found more than two hundred leagues of the land so burnt, so devastated, that land which had been filled with a happy people, that even they, cruel tyrants as they were, looked in horror at the traces left by that first tyrant, on his march into Peru.

The truth of all this has been proved by many witnesses called upon by the Council of the Indies, and their testimony is in the possession of that same Council.[45] Yet never has a single one of those tyrants been burnt at the stake. And their acts of outrageous wickedness that have been proven seem to mean nothing to the ministers of justice who have had to deal with the Indies. Because of their mortal blindness they have never examined the crimes, the ravages and massacres that have been perpetrated and are still being perpetrated by all the tyrant-Governors of the Indies. But they do, now and then, examine the cruelties committed by some knave or other, thus losing to the King some thousands of castellanos, satisfied to argue these little-proven and so very general and confused cases. And they do not even know how to certify these minor cases or reveal, as they should in duty bound to God and the King, the fact that the German tyrants have robbed the King of more than three million castellanos' worth of gold. Because that province of Venezuela, where they ruined and despoiled more than four hundred leagues of land, is the land richest in gold and was the most densely populated of any land in the Indies. And they diverted from the King and wasted more crown revenues in that one kingdom, than the revenues of all the Kings of Spain, a total of millions in the sixteen years since those German tyrants and enemies of God and the King began to occupy that land. And those damages, from now until the end of the world, cannot be remedied unless God by a miracle resuscitates all those thousands of souls that have perished. These are the temporal damages they have caused the King. It would be well to consider what kind and how many damages and dishonors and blasphemies they have perpetrated against God and God's law and what recompense can be made for the countless souls burning in hell because of the greed and inhumanity of those bestial German tyrants.

And now, as to the inhumanity and ruthlessness of those tyrants, I will conclude with this statement. From the time they entered the land until today, they have sent many shiploads of captive Indians to sell them as slaves in Santa Marta, Hispaniola, Jamaica, and the island of San Juan. More than one million Indians. And they continue to do this, the transaction seen and known but dissimulated by the Royal Audiencia of Hispaniola, which hitherto has favored such crimes committed by the tyrants on the islands and on the mainland which they have penetrated for a distance of four hundred leagues, subjecting the mainland Venezuela and Santa Marta. Yet their actions on the mainland could still be checked and remedied. These Indians have given no cause to be enslaved. It is only because of blind perversity and the determination to satisfy their insatiable greed that these avaricious tyrants act as they have acted in the Indies. This alone impels them to take captive meek and innocent people from their houses, separating husbands from wives, fathers from sons, and to brand them with the royal seal and to sell them as slaves.

THAT PART OF THE MAINLAND CALLED FLORIDA

Into these mainland provinces have gone three tyrants at different times from the year one thousand five hundred and ten or eleven, to commit the nefarious acts that have been committed by other tyrants, especially two of them, in other parts of the Indies, so as to rise in rank beyond their merits.[46] And all three tyrants have come to a bad end, losing their lives and possessions, the houses they built in other times with the blood and sweat of the Indians, and their memory is erased from the earth as if they had never lived. They left the entire world scandalized and their names have become a byword of horror and infamy. God ended their lives before they could do more harm. And God has punished them for the evil deeds they committed, deeds I know about, having seen them with my own eyes.

The fourth and the latest tyrant-Governor[47] was appointed with a great to-do in this year one thousand five hundred and thirty-eight. Nothing has been heard of him for three years but we are sure that if he is still alive, wherever he has gone he will have inflicted many cruelties, will have destroyed many nations, for he is of the same breed as those who have ravaged and destroyed most provinces and perpetrated most vile deeds, along with his comrades, but we believe still more strongly that God may have given him the same ending to his life that He gave the other tyrants.

Three or four years after writing the above, I learn that those tyrants who conquered Florida have departed that land, leaving behind them their dead leader. He had committed unheard-of cruelties, which his inhuman comrades repeated against those innocent and harmless peoples. Thus my surmise has been proven not to have been false. His vile deeds were too many and too terrible to recount. I will only reaffirm what I said at the beginning, to wit: The more the conquerors discover new lands, the more lands and peoples do they destroy and with ever greater iniquities against God and man. It is wearisome to dwell on their bloody deeds, the deeds not of men but of wild beasts. I will not tell of their cruelties in detail, but will only relate as an example the following.

On these lands lived a population that was wise, well disposed, politically well organized. As usual, the tyrants perpetrated massacres with the aim of instilling and spreading terror. They afflicted, they killed the people, they took captives and compelled them to carry intolerable loads, like beasts of burden. And when one of the burden-bearers sank under the load, they cut off his head at the neck-chain, so as not to interrupt the march of the others, since they were all chained together, and as I have related above, the head fell to one side of the road, while the body fell to the other.

When the conquerors entered a town, they were greeted cheerfully and were given all the food they required and were assigned six hundred Indians to carry their loads and attend to their horses for their journeys into the interior.

A relative of the leading tyrant returned unexpectedly

from one of these journeys to rob and slay all these people who had thought themselves secure, and he killed with his pike the ruler of the land and committed many other atrocities.

In another village where the people appeared to be more reserved and grudging and were so, because of what they had heard about the horrible acts of the Spaniards, they put all the people to the sword, men, women, and children, young and old, chieftains and subjects, for they spared no one.

Then there was the time when they summoned a great number of Indians, more than two hundred, from another village, or perhaps they came of their own accord. The Spaniards cut their faces from the nose and lips down to the chin and sent them in this lamentable condition, streaming with blood, to carry the news of the miraculous things being done by the Spaniards, advocates of the holy Faith of baptized Catholics. And judge, then, how those people felt, how much love they could have for the Christians, and how they could believe in a God who considered such things good and just, or in the religion the Spaniards professed or in the immaculate Faith of which they boasted. Very great and strange were the evil deeds committed there by those wretched men, children of perdition. And thus, the worst of those wretches, the captain-general, died as if by accident, without confession, and thus no doubt he is now deep in the infernal regions suffering eternal torment, unless perhaps God in His infinite mercy intervenes to ease his punishment, an undeserved relief, considering his execrable misdeeds.

THE RIO DE LA PLATA

As early as the year one thousand five hundred and twenty-two or -three, the Spaniards went to the Rio de la Plata, where are great kingdoms and provinces, inhabited by very well-disposed and reasonable people. Three or four great captains went there. Generally speaking, we know they injured the people and committed murders, but as to particulars, since our information is very much at secondhand, we have little of note to relate. However there is no doubt but that they have done and are still doing the same things they have done elsewhere, in the Indies, since those Spaniards were in other parts where dastardly deeds were perpetrated. And they will become rich and powerful like the others, and this can come about only through the perdition and massacres and subjection of the Indians, according to the way all tyrants think and act.

After having written the above, we have learned very reliably that they have left great provinces devastated in that land, that they perpetrated strange and cruel acts, massacring those unfortunate peoples, that they have conducted themselves even worse than the others, being farther from Spain, that they have behaved with greater injustice than in any other part of the Indies we have described.

Among countless other acts that have been read in the Council of the Indies, we will repeat the following.

A tyranical Governor[48] ordered some of his men to go to a certain village of the Indians for food, telling them that if the Indians refused their request, they were to be killed. The men, with this authority, put to the sword more than five thousand souls, the Indians having refused, more out of fear of the hairy enemy than because of a lack of liberality. Another item. A certain number of peaceful Indians came to offer their services, having been sent for. But since they had not come promptly enough, or else because the Spaniards, as usual, wanted to instill horrible fear in the population, they were turned over to an enemy nation of Indians. Weeping and wailing, the Indians besought the Spaniards to kill them rather than turn them over to their traditional enemies. And these Indians, having come into the house of the Spaniards and refusing to leave, were all put to the sword. As they were killed, they cried out: "We came in peace to serve you, and you kill us! Our blood splattered on these walls will remain as witness to our unjust death and to your cruelty!" This act was certainly a noteworthy one in the annals of Spanish cruelty.

PERU

In the year one thousand five hundred and thirty-one a great tyrant with a company of Spaniards invaded the kingdom of Peru,[49] impelled by the intentions and principles shared by all the other tyrants for he was one of those who had practiced during the longest time all the cruelties and ravages perpetrated on the mainland from the year one thousand five hundred and ten. In Peru the cruelties multiplied and intensified. Massacres and robberies occurred without rhyme or reason. Entire settlements were destroyed, the population was reduced, and so many afflictions were imposed upon this country that we are certain no one would be able to list them, from now until the Day of Judgment. And in truth, the circumstances and quality of those cruel acts cannot be exaggerated.

Upon his invasion of Peru, this tyrant destroyed towns, killed and robbed the people of quantities of gold. On an island near this province, by name Pugna,[50] a beautiful and densely populated place, the Spaniards were welcomed by the ruler and his people as if they were angels from Heaven. Then, after six months there, when they had consumed all the food of the people, they learned there were granaries where the people stored supplies for the times of drought to feed themselves and their families. The Spaniards demanded those supplies and the people brought them, with lamentations at seeing their reserve food wasted, while the Spaniards ate all they liked. The people were repaid by being slain with swords and pikes, or captured and sold as slaves. This act of cruelty and many others had almost depopulated the island by the time the Spaniards left it.

From this island they went to the province of Tumbala[51] on the mainland, where they killed and destroyed all they could. And when the people fled from the tyrant's swords and horrible oppressions, he declared them to be in rebellion against the King of Spain.

This tyrant carried out an ingenious practice. To those he asked for gold or to those who came with presents of gold and silver and whatever possessions they had, he asked them to bring more and when he saw that they had no more or would bring no more, he told them that he would receive them as vassals of the King of Spain, and he embraced them and had the trumpets sound, letting them understand that from then on he would ask for nothing. But he told them that everything they had given him, and everything he had taken or destroyed up to then was justified, now that he had taken them under his protection, and was his by right.

Later on, the native ruler of all these mainland provinces came with his numerous attendants. His name was Atubaliba,[52] and he and his followers were all naked and carried only mock weapons, knowing nothing of swords and pikes, how they could wound, knowing nothing about horses, how they could run, or of what kind of men were these Spaniards who would attack and set upon them demons, if need be, to rob them of gold.

This native King arrived and called out: "Where are these Spaniards? Let them come out, for I will not move from here until they recompense me for the vassals they have taken from me or killed, and for the towns they have destroyed and the wealth they have taken from me!"

The Spaniards came out and assaulted his followers, killing many, after which they captured the ruler who had been borne in state on a litter. They bargained with him for his ransom. He promised to give them gold worth four million castellanos. And he gave them fifteen millions' worth. Upon which, they promised to release him, but they did not keep their promise (as they never did with the Indians in the Indies). Instead, they took him to his people so he could command them to assemble, for he had told them that no leaf on any tree anywhere stirred without his command, but if the people assembled, believing it was at his command, he feared they would slay him.

Despite all this, they condemned him to be burned alive, although some more merciful Spaniards implored the captain to strangle him before burning him. As he heard his sentence pronounced, this Indian ruler asked, "Why will you burn me? What have I done? Did you not promise to release me if I gave you gold? And did I not give you more than you asked for? But since this is what you want, then send me to your King." And he said many other things of this kind, in confusion and revolt against the great injustice of the Spaniards. And finally they burned him.

Consider here the justice and merit of this war against the Indians, the capture of this great ruler and his sentence and execution; consider the behavior of these great tyrants and the rich treasures they took from that powerful chieftain and from other great people of the realm, or the countless wicked and cruel deeds committed in exterminating these peoples, and committed by men who call themselves Christians.

I will now mention a few such actions that were witnessed by a Franciscan friar at the beginning of the invasion of Peru, and which he set down in writing, signing his name. He sent this report in translations to various parts of the Castilian kingdoms. One of them, signed by him, is in my possession, and I will quote from it.

I, the undersigned, Fray Marcos de Niza, of the Franciscan Order called Friars Minor, Father Superior of the said friars, in the province of Peru, who was one of the first religious to accompany the first Christian conquerors of the said province, do state

115

and bear witness to the truth of what I saw with my own eyes in that land, mainly concerning the treatment and conquest of the native peoples.

To begin with, I am a witness with a certain knowledge and experience of the Indians, and I can assert that the Indians of Peru are the most benevolent and kindly disposed to the Christians that I have ever seen. I saw that they gave generously to the Spaniards gold and silver and precious stones and everything they possessed when asked for, all of them being ready to serve and never hostile, always peaceful so long as they were not given occasion by cruel treatment to be warlike, receiving the Spaniards into the villages with generosity and honor, giving them food and what slaves male and female they required.

Furthermore, I bear witness that without cause or occasion, the Spaniards upon entering the lands of the Indians and after their cacique, Atabaliba, had given the Christians more than two millions' worth of gold and all the land he possessed, without resistance, the said cacique was burnt alive.

Atabaliba was the ruler of the entire land, and in pursuit of him, they burned alive his captain–general, Cochilimaca, who had come in peace to the Spanish Governor, in the company of other nobles. And within a few days the Spaniards burned him and Chamba, another noble of the Quito province, who had given no cause, was guilty of no act against them.

Furthermore, they burnt alive Chapera, a lord of the Canaries, again unjustly. They even took Albia, the greatest of the nobles in Quito and, after torturing him in many ways to persuade him to tell where the gold of Atabaliba was hidden, which he could not do because it seems he did not know, they burned his feet. Likewise in Quito they burned Cozopanga, the ruler of all the dependencies of Quito. He had come in peace, at the command of Sebastién de Benalcázar, a captain of the Spanish Governor, and because he did not give the great quantity of gold asked for, they burned him and a number of other nobles and caciques. And *as far as I was able to ascertain, the Spaniards did this with the intention of leaving no prince or chieftain alive in the entire country.*

Furthermore, when the Spaniards had collected a great deal of gold from the Indians, they shut them up in three big houses, crowding in as many as they could, then set fire to the houses, burning alive all that were in them, yet those Indians had given no cause nor made any resistance. And it happened there that a clergyman, Ocaña by name, snatched a boy from the fire, but another Spaniard took him and flung him back into the flames where he was reduced to ashes. And that Spaniard who had flung the boy into the flames dropped dead on the way back to the captain–general's tent. And I was the one who saw to it that he was not given burial.

Furthermore, I affirm that with my own eyes I saw Spaniards cut off the nose, hands, and ears of Indians, male and female, without provocation, merely because it pleased them to do it, and this they did in so many places that it would take a long time to recount. And I have seen Spaniards urge their dogs to tear the Indians to pieces, this I have seen many times. Likewise I have seen the Spaniards burn so many houses and villages that I would be unable to give the number. I have also seen the Spaniards take suckling infants by the arms and fling them as far away as they could, and have seen other outrages and cruelties perpetrated without reason, which filled me with horror, so many that it would take too long to recount.

Likewise, I saw how they summoned the caciques and the chief rulers to come, assuring them safety, and when they peacefully came, they were taken captive and burned. And in my presence they burned two Indians, and although I preached against it I was unable to prevent it. And God knows, and as far as I can comprehend, the uprising of the Indians in Peru occurred for no other reason than because of such outrages and the many other causes the Spaniards gave them. Nor did the Spaniards ever keep their word, but instead, without any reason and unjustly and tyranni-cally, they destroyed the Indians, their lands, their properties, committing such acts that the Indians preferred to die rather than endure them.

Moreover, I can say from having heard the Indians relate it, there is much more gold hidden than displayed, but which, be-cause of their maltreatment, they will not reveal while they are so maltreated. They prefer to die, as others have died before them. And in the said maltreatments, Our Lord has been offended and our King betrayed and defrauded, for this land could easily provide food for all Castile, but it would be very difficult to recuperate the land now, it seems to me.

All the above words are those of the Franciscan Father Superior, and they came to me from the Bishop of Mexico, signed by him, testifying to the fact that they were affirmed by the said Franciscan, Fray Marcos de Niza.

Now, consider what this holy Father says he witnessed, because he traveled through fifty or a hundred leagues of this land and was there from the beginning, for nine or ten years, when very few religious accompanied the four or five thousand Spaniards who invaded Peru, attracted by the smell of gold, and they swept through many great kingdoms and provinces, which they have now destroyed and laid waste in perpetrating the acts which I have related, and many others even more savage and cruel. Truly, they have until now destroyed a thousand times more souls than I have recounted, and with ever less fear of God and of the King and piety, for they have wiped out a great portion of the human family. They have killed in these realms within ten years more than four million souls, and are still killing.

A few days ago they tortured with sharpened reeds and then killed a great queen, the wife of the Inca, King of all these realms which the Christians seized and laid waste. And they took the queen, his wife, and against all justice and reason killed her, even though it is said that she was with child, for the sole reason to cause suffering to her husband.

If an attempt were made to recount in detail the cruel actions and the massacres the Christians have perpetrated and each day are perpetrating in Peru, that relation would be such that all we have recounted of their actions in other parts of the Indies would seem as nothing, by comparison, both in quality and quantity.

THE NEW KINGDOM OF GRANADA

In the year one thousand five hundred and thirty-nine many tyrants combined forces and went from Venezuela and Santa Marta and Cartagena in Peru and from Peru itself to invade and overrun the country adjacent to Santa Marta and Cartagena, which is called The New Kingdom of Granada.[53] They took three hundred leagues of the interior land comprised of flourishing and admirable provinces, inhabited by peaceable and good people like the others elsewhere, and very rich in gold and the precious stones called emeralds. To these provinces the Spaniards applied the name The New Kingdom of Granada, because the first tyrant to arrive there was a native of Granada in Castile.

And since the numerous company of men who acted jointly to conquer this land were the same beasts who had shed blood in other parts of the Indies, they were experts in the horrible crimes I have described, the demoniacal actions they took here were so many and so hideous in both quality and circumstance that they went far beyond all the vile actions committed elsewhere.

Of the countless wicked actions perpetrated by the Spaniards during the three years they occupied The New Kingdom of Granada, I will refer only to a few, and briefly.

An Inquiry was made against a certain Governor who would not acknowledge his vile acts of robbery and murder here, and the eyewitness accounts of his excesses are in the archives of the Council of the Indies. The witnesses all agree that the Indians in this kingdom were peaceable and rendered many services to the Spaniards, bringing them food, the product of their labors, and giving them quantities of gold and the precious stones called emeralds. And they tell how the Spaniards divided up among themselves the people of the villages and their nobles, according to the system of *encomienda*. Thus the Indians were subjected to the condition of slavery. Then the captain–general who had been appointed Governor of the province seized the lord and King of the entire region and held him prisoner for six or seven months, demanding gold of him.

The said King, who was called Bogotá, impelled by fear and hoping to be released, promised to give the Spaniards a house of gold, and he sent Indians to fetch gold and they brought a large quantity. But since he had not kept his promise of a house of gold the Spaniards said they would kill him. The tyrant Governor considered this to be just and sentenced the King to be tortured. First they applied the torture of the screws, then they poured hot candle grease on his belly, then they put his feet in irons through which a stick was thrust that could be twisted, then they set a fire at his feet, and while he was being tortured the Governor came into the room from time to time and told the victim that if he did not keep his promise of giving them a house of gold they would kill him by slow torture.

And it was done. They tortured that King to death. And during the King's torments, God manifested His displeasure by setting afire the entire village where this was taking place.

All the other Spaniards, in imitation of their good leader, used various kinds of refined tortures on the caciques and chieftains of the towns that had been allocated to them (in the system known as the *encomienda*), although the said nobles had given them all the gold and emeralds they had to give, and the tortures were applied only to obtain still more gold and emeralds. And thus they destroyed by burning and other tortures all the nobles of the realm.

Because they were afraid of becoming the victims of the egregious cruelties of one of these tyrants, some Indians fled to the mountains, led by a noble called Daitama. The Spaniards called this a rebellious uprising, and when the Governor heard of it he sent reinforcements to the notorious captain and they marched against the refugees and cut them to pieces, men, women, and children, sparing no one, killing some fifty souls in all. This, although according to some witnesses, the chieftain, Daitama, had brought to the tyrant gold worth four or five thousand castellanos.

On another occasion, when many Indians had come to place themselves peacefully and humbly at the service of the Spaniards, the captain–general came to the town one night and commanded that all those Indians, while they slept, resting from their day's labor, be put to the sword. And this was done, because the captain thought this was the way to maintain fear in the people of this land.

Still another instance. The same captain ordered the Spaniards to take all the caciques and nobles and common people that had been allocated to them and lead them to the town plaza, assuring them of safety. And when this was done he ordered his soldiers to cut off the heads of those Indians. This was done, and in that massacre perished four or five hundred souls. And the witnesses state that the captain considered that such actions would pacify the country.

The witnesses said of a certain tyrant that he perpetrated many acts of cruelty, and mentioned that he cut off the noses and hands of men and women alike, and destroyed many nations.[54]

On one occasion that same cruel man sent out a captain with a company of Spaniards to the province of Bogotá, with the assignment to make enquiries as to who was the noble successor as ruler of the province since the execution by torture of Bogotá, the supreme ruler. They marched through many leagues of the province, capturing for questioning as many Indians as they could. And when a captive Indian did not give the desired information, they cut off his hands or threw him to their savage dogs to be torn to pieces. In this way they destroyed many people.

One day at dawn, the same cruel tyrant ordered his underlings to attack all the caciques and chieftains who had hidden in the mountains but had after a time returned to their villages, having been assured by the Spaniards that they would be unmolested. In this way a great many men and women were captured. These were ordered to place their hands on the ground, which they did, trusting in the good faith of the Spainards. The tyrant then ordered his men to cut off the hands of the captives, who were told they were being punished for not telling the name of their new ruler.

Another time, when some Indians would not surrender a casket full of gold, this tyrant sent troops to make war on them and in that war many souls perished. The survivors either had their hands and noses cut off or were thrown to the dogs, to be torn to pieces and devoured.

On still another occasion, some Indians, upon seeing their villages and towns burnt by the Spaniards, fled to a rocky eminence, led by three or four of their nobles, thinking that they would be able to defend themselves in that cliffy place from the Spaniards, who so lacked humanity. The witnesses say there were four or five thousand Indians in that rocky fortress.

The ruthless captain appealed to the famous tyrant-Governor of the region for reinforcements to help him punish severely the Indians who had fled from the "just and necessary" carnage to take refuge in the mountains, and since they deserved the most cruel tortures, a vengeful war must be waged against them. And since the Spaniards are so pitiless, so alien to those innocents who had done no wrong, reinforcements were sent and a company of men went up to that rocky cliff to subject those Indians who were naked and practically without weapons. The Spaniards told the Indians to come out of hiding, that no harm would be done to them. And that vilest of cruel men commanded his troops to take the cliff by force. And those lions and tigers attacked the helpless sheep. The Indians were disemboweled, were run through with swords and pikes, were cut to pieces. In this carnage the Spaniards had used all their strength, and afterward rested a while. Then the captain commanded them to clean out the cliff and to throw down from it any Indian still in hiding. The witnesses say they saw a cloud of Indians being thrown into the abyss. Some seven hundred were thrown down, to be broken on the rocks below.

Then, to satisfy his cruel appetite, the captain had his men search the cliff for any Indians still in hiding, and all were thrown down.

His cruelty still not satisfied, and as if he wanted to augment the horror of his wickedness, the captain commanded that all the Indians who had been taken alive (and each Spaniard in these ravaging operations had the right to choose Indians, male, female, and children, to serve them), should be placed in a house of straw and to set the house afire, burning all within it to death. The Spaniards did this, after selecting a few of the best to serve them. Some forty or fifty perished in the flames, others were thrown to the dogs to be torn to pieces and devoured.

124

This same tyrant went, on another occasion, to a town named Cota, and captured many Indians, among them fifteen or twenty nobles he ordered to be thrown to the dogs. He also had his troops cut off the hands of a great many of these Indians, both men and women, and had them cut off the noses of a number of women and children who were first gagged and bound. All this was done to show the Indians of what he was capable. Seventy pairs of hands were cut off.

The most cruel exploits of this man, enemy of God, could not be enumerated, for they were countless. Nor could they be described, for nothing like them had been perpetrated in those lands, nor anything like them had ever been seen or heard of either in that province or in Guatemala or in any other region where he has been. Because he has been for many years in those parts, destroying those lands and their peoples.

In addition, the witnesses say in this Inquiry, so many acts of great cruelty have been perpetrated by this captain, so many people have been killed by him and are still being killed in the said New Kingdom of Granada and consented to by all those tyrants and destroyers of humankind, that the lands they hold are laid waste and lost forever and that, unless the King order remedial measures to be taken soon, there will be no Indians left to cultivate the soil and the land will be nothing but an empty desert. And they say that all this destruction was carried out with but one aim: to extract gold from the Indians, who have given all they had to the Spaniards, having no more to give.

There are other big provinces bordering on parts of the said New Kingdom of Granada, which are called Popayán and Cali, and three or four others that comprise more than fifty leagues of land, which have been destroyed, laid waste in the way we have described, lands that were once occupied by countless people, lands depopulated with massacres, tortures, pillage, and other outrages. The land was once a happy one and those who come to it now, when they see it destroyed, are filled with great pity and grief, the towns that were once there have been destroyed, burned, and where lived thousands of people there are now perhaps fifty inhabitants, while other towns, totally razed, are empty. And over a surface of a hundred or two or three hundred leagues which once supported a large population, no one now lives, the land stretches empty, burnt, destroyed.

Many other Spaniards finally came to the New Kingdom, from Peru in the regions of Quito, Popayán, and Cali, some of them coming from Cartagena on their way into Peru, still others by way of the San Juan River on the southern coast. Later on all these Spaniards, all evil-doers, came together in a joint effort which destroyed and depopulated more than six hundred leagues of the land, casting all those unbaptized souls into hell. And today they are still afflicting the innocent and unhappy survivors.

And because, as I said at the beginning, it is a rule that the tyranny and misdeeds against innocent and harmless people increase with time, the inhuman actions of the Spaniards at present merit all the fires of hell, all its tortures.

After the killings and atrocities of the wars, they place the survivors in horrible servitude, under the *encomienda* system as I have said above, allocating them to the Spanish devils, some of whom take three hundred, others two hundred or less. Then the commander summons a hundred Indians to come together before him, and they come like sheep, and he commands his soldiers to decapitate thirty or forty of the Indians, and he tells the others: "I will do the same to you if you do not serve me well or if you try to escape." Could anything be uglier, more horrible, more inhuman than this?

Now, in God's name, you who read this, consider what kind of actions are these which surpass every conceivable cruelty and injustice, and whether it is accurate to call such Christians devils and whether it would be any worse to allocate the Indians to devils from hell rather than to allocate them to the kind of Christians who are in the Indies.

But now I am going to tell of another action the Spaniards engage in which is perhaps even more ferocious and infernal than the one I have just recounted, and it still goes on at the present time. As has been said, the Spaniards train their fierce dogs to attack, kill and tear to pieces the Indians. It is doubtful that anyone, whether Christian or not, has ever before heard of such a thing as this. The Spaniards keep alive their dogs' appetite for human beings in this way. They have Indians brought to them in chains, then unleash the dogs. The Indians come meekly down the roads and are killed. And the Spaniards have butcher shops where the corpses of Indians are hung up, on display, and someone will come in and say, more or less,

"Give me a quarter of that rascal hanging there, to feed my dogs until I can kill another one for them." As if buying a quarter of a hog or other meat.

Other Spaniards go hunting with their dogs in the mornings and when one of them returns at noon and is asked "Did you have good hunting?" he will reply, "Very good! I killed fifteen or twenty rascals and left them with my dogs."

I will finish at this point and shall write no more until more news comes of still more egregious wickedness (if that is possible) or until we return to the Indies and see these things with our own eyes as we constantly did for twenty-two years, constantly protesting before God and my conscience. For I believe, no, I am sure that what I have said about such perditions, injuries, and horrible cruelties and all kinds of ugliness, violence, injustice, thefts, and massacres that those men have perpetrated in these parts of the Indies (and are still perpetrating), I am sure that what I have described is only the ten-thousandth part of what has been done, in quality and quantity, by the Spaniards in the Indies, from the beginning until today.

And so that any Christian may have more compassion for those innocent and ruined nations and their plight, so they may feel the pain of guilt and detest still more the greed and ambition and cruelty of the Spaniards in the Indies, let all that I have said be taken for the real truth, along with what I have affirmed, which is that from the discovery of the Indies until today, never in any part of that New World have the Indians done wrong to the Christians without first having been hurt and robbed and betrayed by them. For in the beginning they thought the Christians were immortals who had come down from Heaven, and they welcomed them, until they saw by their works what these Christians were and what they wanted.

Another thing must be added: from the beginning to the present time the Spaniards have taken no more care to have the Faith of Jesus Christ preached to those nations than they would to have it preached to dogs or other beasts. Instead, they have prohibited the religious from carrying out this intention, and have afflicted them and persecuted them in many ways, because such preaching would, they deemed, have hindered them from acquiring gold and other wealth they coveted. And today in all the Indies there is no more knowledge of God, whether He be of wood or sky, or earth, and this after one hundred years in the New World, except in New Spain, where some religious have gone, and which is but a very small part of the Indies. And thus all the nations have perished and are perishing without the sacraments of the Faith.

I, Fray Bartolomé de Las Casas (or Casaus), a Dominican friar, through the mercy of God, was induced to come to this court of Spain to bring about the ending of that inferno in the Indies and the irremediable destruction of souls that were redeemed by the blood of Jesus Christ; and to set up a work that would bring those souls to know their Creator and Savior. I am also here because of the compassion I have for my native land, Castile, that it not be destroyed by God as punishment for the great sins committed by Spaniards devoid of faith. I am also here because there reside in this court certain persons who are zealous for the honor of God and have compassion for the afflictions of their fellow men.

Finished in Valencia this eighth day of December, one thousand five hundred and forty-two, when actually all the force and violence are at their peak, when conditions in the Indies are at their worst, with all the anguish and disasters, all the massacres, looting, and destruction, outrages, and exterminations I have described. They are the lot of the native peoples in every part of the Indies where there are Christian conquerors. Although in some parts the Christian Spaniards are more ferocious and abominable in their behavior, they are a little less so in Mexico, or at least there they dare not commit their vile acts as openly as in other parts of the Indies. And although some justice does prevail there, all the same, an infernal amount of killing is done. I have great hope that our Emperor Charles V will harken to and comprehend the evils and betrayals that afflict that land and its peoples, against the will of God and against the will of His Majesty, deeds still being perpetrated, because until now the truth has industriously been concealed, and it is my hope that His Majesty will abolish the evils and remedy conditions in the New World that God has entrusted to him, as the lover and motivator of justice that he is, and may God protect his glorious and felicitous life and the Imperial State that all-powerful God has given him, to heal the universal Church. And may his royal soul be saved at last, and may he prosper for many years to come on this earth. Amen.

After writing the above, there were promulgated certain laws and ordinances which His Majesty issued from the city of Barcelona, in the year one thousand five hundred and forty-two, the month of November, and from the palace in Madrid, the following year, by which it was ordained that henceforth such evil deeds and sins against God and our fellow men would cease in the New World. And finally, after having made these laws, His Majesty held many councils and conferences with persons of great authority, learning, and conscience and there were debates in the palace of Valladolid and the votes cast were set down in writing, the Counselors keeping close to the law of Jesus Christ, being good Christians. It was ordained that the Spanish conquerors should cease the corruption and the soiling of their hands and souls in robbing the Indians of their treasures.

The laws being published, the makers of the tyrants who were at the court had many transcriptions made of them, and these were sent to diverse parts of the Indies. (They did this unwillingly, for the laws seemed to shut them out of participating in the robberies and tyrannies.)

And those who, in the Indies, had charge of the ruin and the robberies have continued, as if no orders had been issued, being inspired by Lucifer, when they saw the transcriptions, to engage in still more disorders before the new judges should arrive to execute the laws. And the tyrants rioted and rebelled when the new judges did come to supplant those who had aided and abetted the tyrants (since they had lost all love and all fear of God, and lost all shame and all obedience to the King). And thus they agreed to adopt the fame of traitors, their extreme cruelties and tyrannies were now unleashed, especially in the kingdom of Peru, where today in the year one thousand five hundred and forty-six they are committing such horrible, frightful, nefarious acts as were never before committed in the Indies or anywhere else in the world.

And these acts were committed not only against the Indians, most of the Indians having been killed and their lands destroyed, but against each other, and since the laws of the King no longer operated, punishment came from Heaven, allowing each tyrant to be the executioner of the other.[55]

In imitation of this rebellion against the King in this part of the Indies, the tyrants in other parts of the New World have disregarded the new laws and are behaving in the same way. For they cannot bring themselves to relinquish the estates and properties they have usurped, or let go their hold on the Indians, whom they maintain in perpetual subjection. And wherever killing with the sword has come to an end, they are killing the Indians little by little through subjecting them to servitude. And until now the King has been powerless to check them, for all the Spaniards, young and old, in the Indies, are occupied in pillage, some openly, others secretly and stealthily. And with the pretense of serving the King they are dishonoring God and robbing and destroying the King.

translated from the Spanish by Herma Briffault

NOTE ON THE TRANSLATION
OF THE *BREVISSIMA RELACION*

LAS CASAS's sentences are sometimes terribly long, and since he uses practically no conjunctions except "and," one loses the thread before reaching the end, where sometimes the verb is to be found. I have slightly broken up the sentences and have occasionally used "but," "although," etc. to make the meaning clearer. Las Casas's biggest "sin" aside from some exaggeration is his repetitiveness. Sometimes in the course of a long sentence he repeats what he had said at the beginning; and also repeats on a later page what he had said earlier. I have eliminated most of the repetitions.

My aim, which I hope I have reached, was to preserve the 16th century feeling in the English prose, while still making it accessible to the modern reader. Occasionally, to preserve Las Casas's style, I have kept his loose constructions, but have not done so consistently.

Herma Briffault

NOTES

THE DEVASTATION OF THE INDIES: A BRIEF ACCOUNT

1. India—*Las Indias*—was what the Spanish discoverers called the islands in the Carribean and the coasts of Central and South America, being as we know under the misapprehension of having found the sea route to India.

2. Hispaniola—Small Spain—or Haiti is the Carribean island that comprises the Dominican Republic and the Republic of Haiti.

3. A *vara* is a unit of length about 2.4 ft.

4. San Juan is the old name of the Island of Puerto Rico.

5. The Lucayos and Gigantes comprise today's Bahamas.

6. Meant is Pedro de Ysla, a trader. His name has come down to us in one of Las Casas's other writings.

7. A Spanish *legua* comprises roughly 3½ miles.

8. "Come and behold the men who have stepped down from heaven, and bring them food and drink." According to Columbus' ship's diary

these were the words uttered by the inhabitants of the Antilles upon first greeting the Spaniards. The Mayas and Aztecs, too, regarded the Europeans as of supernatural descent—because of their height, their skin color and their beards.

9. At the time of the conquest the West Indies knew neither dogs nor horses. The Spaniards created terror with their animals and made the Indians' fear of these animals useful to themselves psychologically and militarily.

10. 4.5 grams of gold was the quivalent of a *castellano* in the West Indies which did not have a mint during the time of the conquest.

11. The "admiral" is Columbus. The episode described here is also confirmed in Fernando Columbus' *Historia.*

12. "Their memory," Las Casas says of the leaders of the Conquista, "has now been eliminated from the face of the earth, as though they had only belonged to the living." He is thus consistent in not naming any of them, as though to eliminate them also from human history. In this Las Casas did not succeed; which is not surprising, for history cannot be written without naming its criminals. That is why we identify them whenever possible, for those who wish to know their names. The governor of Hispaniola referred to here was Nicolas de Ovando.

13. An *arroba* equals roughly 22 pounds.

14. This commander was a certain Pánfilia de Narváez.

15. The man was called Roderige Albuquerque.

16. This governor of Darien was Pedro Arias d'Avila. According to Ovieda he was responsible for the death of roughly two million people.

17. Darien was what the Spanish called the present border area between the Republics of Panamá and Colombia.

18. New Spain is today's México.

19. Those chiefly responsible for the massacre of Mexico are the Governor of Cuba Diego de Velásques and his secretary Hernán Cortéz.

20. It was a case of settling accounts. Diego de Veláques tried to bring down Cortéz, using the aforementioned Pánfilio de Narváez for this purpose. Cortez came out the stronger.

21. According to Prescott, in *The Conquest of Mexico,* the Indians were celebrating their war god and their dance was a war dance.

22. Pánuco is today's Tampico; Colima is a Mexican state on the

Pacific coast. The other names should presumably be read as Tutupepec and Chilpanicingo. The criminals in question are Francisco de Garay, Governor of Jamaica, and Captain Gonzales de Sandoval.

23. Those responsible were Pedro de Alvarado and Cristóbal de Olid.

24. Utitlan, the old capital of Quiché, was situated near today's border between México and Guatemala.

25. This town is called Antigua today.

26. One quintal weighed 200 pounds.

27. Pedro de Alvarado was crushed to death by his own horse. Cristóbal de Olid was murdered by his confrères.

28. The person in question is a certain Francisco de Garay.

29. The *Audiencia Real* was a local office of the Royal Council in Madrid. In the American colonies it was the highest Spanish administrative authority.

30. Meant is today's state of Michoacán which lies southwest of México City.

31. The culprit was the first Governor of Pánuco, Nuno de Guzman.

32. Xalisco is called Jalisco today and is one of the federal states of Mexico.

33. Zechariah XI: 4,5.

34. This governor was a certain Francisco Montejo who achieved particular reknown because he fed Indian children to his dogs.

35. Francisco Montejo.

36. 2 Kings 17, 21. Las Casas quotes the Latin: *peccare fecit Israel.*

37. A province in the farthest northeast of Colombia.

38. The guilty: Alfonso de Ojeda, Pedro de Villafuerte, Juan de Ampues, Gonzales Ximenes de Quesada and Garcia de Lerma.

39. Paria is a peninsula in northeast Venezuela. The Gulf of Venezuela is called Lago de Maracaibo today. Coast of Pearls is the old name of the beach between Caracas and the peninsula.

40. This city today is called Higüerote.

41. Island of Pearls—Isla de Margarita.

42. The Yuya Pari is identical with the Orinoco. The conquistador referred to here—Diego de Ortaz—was poisoned by his confrères.

43. The Augsburg banking house of Welser financed the election in 1519 which made Charles V emperor. The Welsers also financed the

Spanish crown's overseas expeditions. In exchange Charles V made over to Bartholomäus Welser in 1526 the province of Venezuela for him to exploit it as he pleased. This gift was withdrawn again in 1545, presumably because of the influence of the present report.

Welser sent four representatives to Venezuela. Three hundred Spanish mercenaries were hired for the expedition. Their commander was a certain Ambrosius Dalfinger from Ulm.

44. Meant is a legendary palace in Peru which was supposedly made of pure gold and inhabited by the golden king, *el dorado.* The palace was never found.

45. The Indian Council, *Consejo de las Indias* or *Concilium Indianum,* the highest legal authority for the American colonies, had its seat in Madrid. Its branch offices were called *Audiencias Reales.*

46. One of the chief culprits is already familiar from the report: namely Pánfilio de Narváez. The two others were called Juan Ponce de León and Alvar Nunez Cabeza de Vaca.

47. The history of the conquest honors this man to this day. He was called Hernando de Soto.

48. This refers to a certain Pedro de Mendoza.

49. The culprit's name was Francisco Pizarro. His accomplices were Diego d'Almagro and Hernando de Soto.

50. The Island Puná lies in the Pacific in front of Guayaquil in Ecuador.

51. What is being referred to is Tumbes, a town in the north of Peru.

52. Atabaliba, Atahualpa in today's transcription, was the 13th king of the Incas.

53. The colony of Granada comprised the interior of today's Colombia, that is chiefly the plateau of Bogotá. The responsible governor is already known to us—Gonzales Ximenes de Quesada.

54. This servant of the Spanish crown was a certain Sebastián de Balalcazar.

55. Pizarro had his accomplice Diego d'Almagro choked to death; three years later he was liquidated by d'Almagro's followers. Poisonings, mutual denunciations and executions, even regular crusades of the conquistadores against each other were quite customary in Spanish America.